by Mike Benson, Terry B
William Buckingham, Rory Canellis, Mike Cox,
Paul DiMarzio, George Galambos, Daniel Kaberon,
Mike Kearney, Terry Keene, Martin Kennedy,
Bill Mitlehner, Bill O'Donnell, Carl Parris,
Gary Puchkoff, Joseph Temple, Robert Vaupel,
Chris Vignola, Maryela Weihrauch, Steve Wood,
Brian Woods, Les Wyman

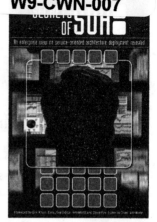

W9-CWN-007

TRADEMARK DISCLAIMER:

Trade names and trademarks referred to within this book are the property of their respective trademark holders. None of these trademark holders are affiliated with Larstan Publishing, this book or its web sites.

Published by:
Larstan Publishing Inc.
10604 Outpost Dr., N. Potomac, MD 20878
240-396-0007 ext. 901
www.larstan.com

PRINTED IN THE UNITED STATES OF AMERICA

10 9 8 7 6 5 4 3 2 1

Design by Rob Hudgins and 5050Design.com
Front and back cover designed by Mike Gibson of
The Love Has No Logic Design Group (http://www.lovehasnologic.com)

ISBN, Print Edition 978-0-9776895-7-6
Library of Congress Control Number: 2006930680
First Edition

This book is designed to provide accurate and authoritative information on the topic of service-oriented architecture. It is sold with the understanding that neither the Authors nor the Publisher are engaged in rendering any professional or consulting services by publishing this book. As each individual situation is unique, questions relevant to service-oriented architecture should be addressed to an appropriate professional to ensure that the situation has been evaluated carefully and appropriately. The Authors and Publisher specifically disclaim any liability, loss or risk which is incurred as a consequence, directly or indirectly, of the use and application of any of the contents of this work.

FOREWORD

Everyone has heard the clichés about "aligning business and IT," as if technologists needed to be corralled into serving business needs. The problem, though, isn't the will; it's the way.

SOA (service-oriented architecture) provides the means for IT to meet today's urgent demand for a new level of agility. At its heart, SOA is a set of general design principles that enables organizations to change business processes on the fly and respond to the shifting demands of the business in a manner that would be impractical or cost-prohibitive using conventional application development and resource allocation.

In an attempt to lock in the potential benefits of reduced IT costs and greater business agility, most large enterprises now have SOA initiatives underway. Indeed, over the past few years, *InfoWorld* has interviewed dozens of enterprise officers, architects and developers who are guiding their organizations toward SOA deployment—and who are learning hard lessons, gaining insight and encountering infuriating technology gaps along the way. Many are already enjoying SOA's early benefits of easy integration and code reusability.

Yet even when the payback is not as immediate, SOA enjoys extraordinary traction for another reason: In contrast to other "big bang" endeavors, a service-oriented architecture doesn't require organizations to discard their current applications and infrastructure. Nor does it threaten to freeze business processes in place, as many of the old-fashioned, monolithic applications do. The ultimate objective is to enable composite application development, where IT can meet the needs of business by stringing together services into process-driven

applications, rather than hard-coding business processes that will be out of date next month or next year.

Given such potential, it's not surprising that many organizations are already provisioning the services fundamental to their business, beginning with domain areas where quick response to the whims of customers, partners or markets is essential. Creating policies for building services and governing their use in applications is what SOA is all about. The idea is simple, but the execution isn't, because SOA turns the conventional model of enterprise software development on its head. Normally, programmers write software based on a set of well-defined requirements. SOA demands that organizations create an ecosystem of services that may ultimately have an army of stakeholders inside and outside the firewall. The initial challenge of SOA is knowing where and how to begin—where to draw a box around a fixed set of requirements and how to build services that will yield tangible ROI while keeping an SOA fully extensible.

In most cases, SOA builds on the stack of protocols that define web services, but it is hardly limited to that stack. Most successful SOA implementations draw as much on time-honored notions of business re-engineering as they do on XML, SOAP and WSDL. Think of SOA as a broad, standards-based framework in which new services are created, deployed, governed, orchestrated and recombined so that current and future apps can draw on their power.

Many organizations embarking on the SOA path start by provisioning a few mission-critical legacy applications as services, providing access to important data and functionality to other applications for the first time. Or they use shared services to eliminate redundancy among several difficult-to-maintain stovepipe applications that overlap in functionality.

Such projects may yield significant benefits. SOA delivers the most value, and will scale far better in the future, however, when business stakeholders can identify a set of business problems (and their related business processes) that need streamlining, rather than attacking technology problems first. Once they sketch out an end state describing how the business should work optimally, IT architects can begin mapping that top-down view to the bottom-up reality of existing applications, services and infrastructure.

That architectural vision can result in a harmonious, scalable ecosystem or an unholy mess of point-to-point spaghetti, depending on how an organization plans, builds, deploys and manages. A healthy SOA initiative starts with funding. In the traditional IT funding model, business stakeholders bankroll discrete projects with specific objectives. SOA requires a different approach—a company-wide commitment to technology that will benefit the entire organization. It's a tough sell that requires vision on the part of senior-level management. Because deployment requires a shared infrastructure, initial ROI can be hard to measure. In essence, a leap of faith is required.

Once that commitment has been made, the hard work begins: creating governance—the collection of policies that guides service design and runtime interactions. Governance defines the difference between a collection of web services and SOA. Rather than being retrofitted after the fact, governance must be baked in from the start for any serious SOA deployment.

Clearly SOA goes beyond any single IT project. The idealized (if still largely theoretical) endgame of SOA is an enterprise-wide infrastructure that functions as one giant service-based meta-application, capable of meeting any business requirement.

Hooking up BPM (business process management) to large portions of SOA infrastructure will represent one big step toward that endgame. Another will be wide deployment of integrated BAM (business activity monitoring) solutions, which tap into SOA message streams to help guarantee that processes and composite applications are providing the best possible business value. Beyond those technologies, industry SOA boosters set their sights high, prophesizing a self-optimizing IT nirvana in which applications and network infrastructures monitor and reconfigure themselves based on easily adjusted business rules.

These kinds of grand-scale, self-optimizing SOAs aren't due this decade. With the most advanced of today's enterprises barely achieving orchestration, SOA still needs to fill a few gaps—in security, reliable messaging, semantics, process management and so on—and work its way through important governance issues.

What's just as clear, however, is that SOA is delivering real value now. Early SOA efforts are already establishing new lines of communication between IT and business—and in some cases, beginning to affect the organization of business itself, as people grow to understand how service orientation can eliminate duplicative effort and shorten development time. In these instances, the future is already here.

—Eric Knorr, Executive Editor, InfoWorld *and*
Steve Fox, Editor in Chief, InfoWorld

Chapter

⬜ ⬜ ① ⬜ ⬜

SERVICE-ORIENTED I.T.: THE GOAL IS WITHIN OUR GRASP

Today, one of the hottest, most talked-about innovations within the information technology community is service-oriented architecture. Only time will tell whether or not SOA is the Holy Grail for which technologists have quested. However, this author's convinced the stars really have aligned this time.

BY PAUL DiMARZIO

Computer mavens always seem obsessed with the "Next Big Thing." Problem is, the latest fad in the IT world often turns out to be a technological *cul-de-sac* — it's neither next, nor big, nor even much of a thing.

For the last two decades, a wide variety of IT technologies have emerged that promised to better align the operations of the IT shop with the needs of business. Some never caught on; some succeeded but only in specific segments. Some were wildly popular for a while, only to give way to a new tech trend. But none of them completely fulfilled the promise.

That was then; this is now. The emergence of service-oriented architecture (SOA) may finally achieve the long-frustrated goal of closely matching technological capabilities with business exigencies.

> **DEPLOYMENT DOES INDEED MATTER—IT MATTERS A LOT. SO MUCH SO THAT IT REQUIRES AS MUCH AS, IF NOT MORE, ATTENTION THAN DEVELOPMENT. IN FACT, IT HAS BECOME APPARENT TO ME THAT LARGER AND MORE COMPLEX ENTERPRISES NEED TO TAKE EVEN GREATER CARE TO ENSURE THAT SOA SERVICES ARE DEPLOYED ON PLATFORMS BEST ABLE TO HANDLE THE JOB PROPERLY.**

Much has been written about SOA. Virtually all of the discussion so far has focused on either expected value to the business or the technologies that can be used to transform business processes into a set of networked services defined within an SOA. Curiously, what has been missing is in-depth guidance on deploying those services.

The platform-agnostic nature of SOA *development* technologies has led many pundits who watch this space to follow the path of least resistance and take up a matching platform-agnostic view of SOA *deployment*. Having observed several large enterprises that are reaping the benefits of SOA, as well as others that are struggling, I have concluded that deployment does indeed matter—it matters a lot. So much so that it requires as much as, if not more, attention than development. In fact, it has become apparent to me that larger and more complex enterprises need to take even greater care to ensure that SOA services are deployed on platforms best able to handle the job properly.

INCREASING PRODUCTIVITY AND RESPONSIVENESS

It's not my intent to revisit all the potential business benefits of SOA here, but I do want to explore briefly two important business requirements that are addressed by SOA because they illustrate the tight linkage between achieved business value and the approach taken towards SOA deployment. These are the need to become more productive, and the need to become more responsive. These fundamental requirements manifest in myriad ways, but I will present two specific examples.

Productivity can be defined as a more optimal use of existing people skills, a more effective utilization of financial assets or an increasing skill in husbanding resources. There are others. My focus here is on the productivity gains that can be realized through the reuse of business services.

SOA defines a standard means of describing, discovering and invoking services. In theory, all services within an SOA deployment can become universally and heavily reused, thereby saving on development and maintenance cost and boosting productivity. In practice, however, reuse is only occurring with any degree of regularity today at lower organizational levels such as within departmental applications.

There is not much reuse of services occurring at the business unit or enterprise level where the payback can be much greater. I believe the

Much has been written about SOA. Virtually all of the discussion so far » **SOA SECRET** has focused on either expected value to the business or the technologies that can be used to transform business processes into a set of networked services defined within an SOA.

primary reason is that an SOA service is not inherently and automatically reusable; it often requires additional investment in time and treasure to ensure that the service meets the needs of all potential users, both now and in the future. The cost is certainly greater than zero and can add a significant premium to the development of a non-reusable service (one client has told me that it can cost as much as 60% more in the development budget to make a service reusable). In the end, the return on investment at the enterprise level would justify this additional cost. However, the myopic manner in which software projects are currently funded in most enterprises restricts and can actually discourage developing a software asset that could be reused.

Consider an enterprise where each line of business owns its IT assets and controls funding of development projects on a cost/return basis. Under this model, the organizational goal is to complete projects quickly and inexpensively and the extra cost of reuse is viewed as overhead to be avoided, rather than investment. In a banking enterprise, for example, an online banking group may develop an exception handling service that could be reused by the mortgage group. But there is no business incentive for the online group to make the additional investment necessary to make that happen. Further complicating this issue is that even if the investment was made, there is no policy or internal mechanism for the mortgage group to receive support on a service owned by the online group. There isn't even a guarantee that the service will not be changed incompatibly in the future.

A similar situation exists for *responsiveness*, which can also be defined by many different aspects. It can, for example, be the ability to react to changing customer needs, the ability to capitalize on a new opportunity or the ability to react to problems. From a technological perspective, the ability to map business processes directly to a set of corresponding workflows (as defined by SOA) is a major enabler of responsiveness. This capability, known as process serving, involves a software deployment model where applications are assembled,

deployed and monitored, rather than designed, compiled and run, with the coordination and orchestration of a set of services replacing the fragile call/return model of traditionally developed applications.

Process serving has incremental value when applied within portions of an organization, but its true power and value is best realized across departments at organizational and enterprise levels. For example, it's good to develop processes within the marketing organization, but it's even better to develop processes that span development, marketing and sales so business processes can be coordinated and driven across the entire organization. This is where the real business benefit of SOA is realized.

Just as enterprise reuse requires a new approach towards development funding, the deployment of an enterprise process can also require vastly different characteristics than those of a line-of-business process. At higher levels that cross organizational boundaries, the business value of process serving tends to have a greater degree of dependence on qualities like availability, security and manageability that do not always show a return on investment in a price/performance evaluation. At the department level, deployment of a process would be able to trade off "good enough" quality to derive better price/performance. A department rarely evaluates the non-functional requirements in a manner needed at the enterprise level. Still, most enterprises use a departmental model for this assessment and run the risk of developing sub-par enterprise services.

INFRASTRUCTURE AND CONTROL

The point of this discussion of productivity and responsiveness is to illustrate my belief that the true business value of SOA surfaces only when SOA is managed and deployed with an enterprise perspective. SOA is one of those truly disruptive technologies that occurs every decade or so and literally rewrites the rules for how information technology can be used to further an organization's business goals.

SOA BENEFITS FULLY REQUIRE A FUNDAMENTAL CHANGE IN THE WAY IT INVESTMENTS ARE MADE AND MANAGED. STILL, MOST ORGANIZATIONS CONTINUE TO MAKE SOA DEPLOYMENT DECISIONS USING TRADITIONAL METHODS THAT LIMIT THE BENEFITS OF SOA.

The first mainframes were an example of such a disruptive technology. They have been followed by similarly disruptive technologies such as Intel-based distributed servers, distributed operating systems like Windows, UNIX and Linux, and the Java-centric programming model. All have had a profound and lasting effect on IT practices. However, with SOA, most organizations are still trying to force-fit a decades-old model of IT best practices for infrastructure evaluation into what is, in effect, a radically different technology. To realize SOA benefits fully requires a fundamental change in the way IT investments are made and managed. Still, most organizations continue to make SOA deployment decisions using traditional methods that limit the benefits of SOA.

These observations are becoming standard within the analyst community. According to a recent Forrester Group paper, "the traditional IT organization, which is oriented toward discrete business units and supported by vertically integrated applications, constrains this optimization rather than helps. To be effective, the IT organization must develop an orientation around end-to-end business processes."[1] This position is echoed by a report from the Aberdeen Group that states: "The psychology of IT spending is still oriented towards squeezing as much as possible from the IT budget."[2] The bottom line is that SOA requires an investment approach towards laying down the appropriate infrastruc-

ture for the enterprise, yet the majority of organizations continue to take a traditional price/performance view that argues for the return on investment of smaller-scale efforts.

SOA also requires carefully designed and consistently enforced control mechanisms, or governance, around these infrastructure investments. Dennis Gaughan, an analyst at AMR Research, Inc., points out in a recent *Computerworld* article that the ownership of traditional applications, defined by functional areas, is clearly defined. But with the "tectonic shift" to SOA, there are a lot of questions about who owns the applications. A key element of SOA success, he writes, "is having a crystal-clear understanding of governance, accountability and service-level expectations."[3] The value of governance to the success of SOA cannot be overstated. According to the Gartner Group, "lack of working governance mechanisms in midsize-to-large (greater than 50 services) post-pilot projects will be the most common reason for project failure."[4]

Sadly, it is exactly this understanding of the value of infrastructure and corresponding controls that is missing today and is causing many enterprises to struggle with SOA adoption. Consider the following analogy: In the United States, we recently marked the centennial of the Great San Francisco earthquake, a seminal event in U.S. history. At the start of the 20th Century, San Francisco was a rapidly growing community that gave little thought to the quality of the city's infrastructure. Buildings went up fast and cheap to accommodate rapid growth. The "Big Quake" of 1906 provided a sobering lesson for building on the

---

The bottom line is that SOA requires an investment approach towards » **SOA SECRET** laying down the appropriate infrastructure for the enterprise, yet the majority of organizations continue to take a traditional price/performance view that argues for the return on investment of smaller-scale efforts.

AN ATTITUDE ADJUSTMENT

By Kevin Kelly, Sr. IT Architecture &
Strategy Consultant, Kemar Solutions, Inc.

The notion of a service-oriented architecture is not new, even if the term is. I was first introduced to the concept of service orientation in the late 1960s. (Yes, son, we did have computers in those days.) At that time I was working with Aer Lingus—Irish Airlines—on an International Programmed Airline Reservation System[1] (IPARS) team that implemented an Airlines Control Program (ACP). One of the interesting elements of the system was the notion to reuse modules which were purpose-built as common services with a published service contract.

Reflecting on the early days of service orientation has led me to believe the biggest challenge of SOA is not technological as much as ideological. The technologies now being introduced to support SOA certainly make things easier, but they don't address the heart of the problem. SOA is as much a state of mind as it is a technology. It's as much about behavior and orientation as it is about programming per se. When I came to IPARS at Aer Lingus, the overall orientation was a *fait accompli*; we were introduced to it as the way the system worked. It never occurred to us to vary from that orientation. After all, the common modules which were packaged with the system worked perfectly well; why would we want to replace them with something of our own that would then require extensive testing. It didn't occur to us at the time to wonder if this was the best way forward, any more than it occurs to a carpenter to wonder whether or not he could design screws that are better than what's commercially available. But when it comes to an examination of the philosophy, a few things become apparent.

The SOA State of Mind: First of all, attitude is extremely important when one starts to consider the realm of reuse. This includes the attitude of the developer, who voluntarily agrees to curb the application of his or her innovation to tackling previously unaddressed business problems, rather than to finding different and arguably better ways to address something that has already been done. The decision to reuse is usually a good decision for the enterprise but often a painful decision for the solution builder accustomed to being rewarded for innovation and technical know-how. The attitude of IT management is also important, for it is this element that encourages and rewards reuse. Finally, the attitude of the business owner of an initiative can make or break a program in terms of how much IT flexibility is allowed and undertaken to build and support reusable capability. The enterprise-wide rewards are great, though the immediate cost can be higher. But part of what makes SOA different is that it is done for long-term benefits, rather than the immediate and sole benefit of the primary sponsor.

Service and Serendipity: There is a belief abroad that services can be "discovered," that one can successfully mine one's IT portfolio for those immediately reusable gems. In truth, the likelihood that one can trip over service-oriented components produced by a non-service-oriented development team is abysmally low. Another interesting theory perpetrated by some senior executives is that reusable components will be developed by project teams contracted to address a particular business need, without any additional cost or effort. History indicates that this rarely is realized. The truth is services must be built deliberately, with lots of forethought. They must be designed with a particular intent but also with the broadest possible implications. The testing of a reusable service must also be done in a context broader that that for a non-reusable component, because the simple truth is that over-testing of IT components is rare.

Funding: Developing a reusable service generally costs more than an equivalent non-reusable service. In my experience, most IT application initiatives are funded by interested business areas. They want value for their money as defined by maximum benefit for minimum cost. The fit of reusable services into a minimum cost equation is uncomfortable. The dilemma, then, is who is going to pay the delta cost for delivering a service in a reusable vs. non-reusable form. Should the first user have to pay for what is actually a charitable donation to the rest of the organization? Should a business user who agrees to such an investment somehow be able to recoup the cost from other prospective users? One can imagine a variety of options, but the bottom line is that if the community at large is to be the beneficiary of SOA, the community at large should pay in some manner. The easiest way may be some form of enterprise funding for the delta cost in return for a dedicated or normal project team undertakening all of the development and necessary testing.

Behavior and Culture: One can argue whether culture creates behavior or behavior defines culture. The point is that bringing about "the SOA IT" is largely a question of reinforcing behavior and creating culture. We must reward the behavior (e.g., reuse, common component delivery, etc.) deemed desirable and, if necessary, punish the behavior deemed undesirable. If we preach reuse while rewarding developers who pay no attention to it, we should not be surprised when the majority of developers perceive reuse as unimportant.

Boundaries: The concept of SOA crosses many boundaries surrounding IT. It permits the exploitation of services without regard to location or implementation. I spent many years at RBC Financial Group and one of our earliest examples of service reuse was the exploitation of IMS transactions from an intelligent controller (e.g., IBM 3600) and later PC workstations. In fact, in the early 1980s we implemented a middleware capability to support service-oriented

interaction between a number of different mainframe systems distributed across Canada. In that context, client-server meant any interaction between programmatic entities where "client" and "server" were roles, both of which might be played at different times by the same IMS application. This interaction was a fairly straightforward peer-to-peer relationship based on available mainframe infrastructure and did not require any off-mainframe capability. There's really no philosophical difference between either client and service consumer or server and service provider in this context. The key is to recognize the value you already have and find ways to exploit it through an appropriate form of loose coupling. That value is in application services and also in infrastructure. Business risk also is reduced through reusing something that's already proven rather than building something entirely new.

To return to the Aer Lingus IPARS experience, we started with a critical mass of services and service exploiters which came as part of the system from IBM. Because of this existing critical mass, it was easy to follow the example of our predecessors and continue in the service-oriented vein. It's not so easy when you start trying to introduce SOA to an organization with no experience. It's necessary to have a holistic approach, one which includes organizational, behavioral and attitudinal perspectives. Having a sound technology base will certainly help, but you need more, and it's a slow haul.

Don't be discouraged if your SOA initiative is not an immediate success. Ultimately, it will provide maximum benefit.

---

[1] IPARS was an internationalization of the PARS system developed by IBM and American Airlines. The internationalization work was done by a team located at what was then British Overseas Airways Corporation (BOAC) at London's Heathrow Airport. The team was composed of IBM and airline staff from around the world and I had the opportunity to work there for a time in 1968.

> **SOA PROJECTS CONTINUE TO BE FUNDED AND MANAGED ACCORDING TO A RISK MODEL THAT IS RAPIDLY BECOMING OBSOLETE. SOA REQUIRES AN INVESTMENT APPROACH THAT RECOGNIZES THE CRITICAL IMPORTANCE OF INFRASTRUCTURE. SINCE IT IS EXTREMELY DIFFICULT TO CALCULATE THE RETURN ON AN INFRASTRUCTURE INVESTMENT FOR A SINGLE PROJECT, THESE DECISIONS MUST BE MADE AT THE ENTERPRISE LEVEL.**

cheap. San Francisco learned the hard way the true value of infrastructure and governance. Today, no new construction can occur in the San Francisco Bay area without strict adherence to a tough set of codes designed to prevent the loss of life and preserve critical infrastructure in case of another strong earthquake. Such additional investment in infrastructure and controls is expensive, yet the focus on quality over pure price/performance is deemed necessary.

So what does this have to do with SOA deployment? From my perspective the current approach mirrors the prevalent attitude of boomtown San Francisco of 1906. SOA projects are going up all over the place with a focus on deploying services fast and cheap to accommodate business growth and competitive pressure. In business, as in life, much is uncertain. However, risks can be understood and calibrated to determine the maximum level acceptable and companies can plan accordingly. SOA inherently involves opening critical business systems to a wide variety of new risks, yet SOA projects continue to be funded and managed according to a risk model that is rapidly becoming obsolete. SOA requires an investment approach that recognizes the

critical importance of infrastructure. Since it is extremely difficult to calculate the return on an infrastructure investment for a single project, these decisions must be made at the enterprise level.

The focus of this book then is not about the business value of SOA, or how to develop SOA services, but rather on the value to IT in making enterprise-level SOA infrastructure investments. As Forrester points out, "you must begin to re-architect your IT organization around services and start your IT organization's incremental transformation to support business objectives while making business processes central to your IT organization's design process. This strategic adoption of SOA will fundamentally change the IT department within the business, leading to a service-oriented IT (SO-IT) organization."[5] It is time for the service-oriented IT. Once this approach to SOA is taken, a whole new range of SOA deployment options will be revealed and a more effective means of evaluating them will emerge.

THE REPEAL OF MOORE'S LAW

As SOA is driving the need for IT to refocus its energies at the enterprise level, a parallel disruptive technological trend is also emerging that is having a profound effect on the semiconductor industry: the impending death of "Moore's Law." Moore's Law, named from observations by Intel co-founder Gordon E. Moore, states that computer processing power, as measured by the number of transistors on integrated circuits, doubles every 18 months. Moore's Law is often cited to describe the exponential improvement of processor performance, capacity and function.

> **Enterprises that are most successful in deploying SOA also tend to take an incremental approach, but always within the context of a broader, enterprise-wide plan. They do not try and justify the return on investment at the project level alone.**
>
> » SOA SECRET

OVERCOMING BASIC BARRIERS TO SOA

ANOTHER VIEW

By Keith Harris, VP Retail Architecture and Integration, Wachovia

When a company enters the world of service-oriented architecture, it must invest in more than technology. It must be committed to changing the way people perceive the applications, servers and other IT investments that make products and services—and, ultimately, SOA—possible.

For starters, the enterprise must ensure that employees have the appropriate training in both SOA and relevant supporting technologies, such as web services, XML and security. People also should be trained in governance and processes, and truly understand how components and developing shared common modules fit into an SOA framework.

Enterprises also must recognize that other ways of doing business may need to change, as well. Many large companies—the ones most likely to invest in this concept—have historically built budgets in isolation; therefore, these budgets led to silo projects and silo IT implementations and, ultimately, to silo hardware and software implementations. The result is a silo architecture and its accompanying redundancies in applications and infrastructure. One day these companies often look up to find they have numerous redundant functions, such as a bank having four, five or even six credit engines.

Supporting these silos are physical servers, many of them built for each individual solution and organized into little farms. The result for many: server sprawl. Over the years, some organizations have accumulated thousands of servers and are adding hundreds of new ones every month. In these configurations, it is common to see

each application having its own set of infrastructure and running at extremely low utilization.

For many large organizations it is difficult to meet all the requirements for a shared service implementation. A major process problem is project alignment. Project teams all have different timelines and separate budgets and don't want to stop or slow down to understand and incorporate an aggregate set of commonly shared services. Overcoming this inertia can be quite problematic. It requires new processes and new governance to avoid redundant SOA services. Otherwise, people will just turn around and continue building redundant services—only this time in an SOA way. And at the end of the day, they'll have accomplished nothing.

Another critical governance adjustment is in how SOA impacts the definition of an application. Shared components are used to the point no one owns all the pieces and parts that comprise an application. Gartner calls this a "composite application." This process begins to break down some of those ownership barriers. It also impacts contracts and service-level agreements (SLAs) that have to be put into place around these SOA components. No longer can the agreements be measured across the entire application level, but they must now be addressed at the component level. Since each application is using shared components, and the SLAs are created around these components, the question becomes: Who supports the components and not the component application?

On the technology side, when a company is moving towards SOA it must have platforms that leverage hardware and OS virtualization. Without that there will be server sprawl. SOA ultimately demands bullet-proof platforms that can leverage hardware and OS virtualizations. It must be stressed that when services are being shared across multiple systems, the infrastructure the SOA service sits on

has to be bullet-proof because now, if it goes down, it's not just one application that's impacted. Instead, a domino effect will cause multiple lines of business to suffer simultaneously. To avoid this, SOA infrastructure has to reach new levels of scalability and maintainability. Without that, the whole concept of shared components breaks down.

Beyond the need for rock-solid infrastructure, SOA provides applications with enhanced flexibility and agility. Many companies will begin their SOA journey with an initial goal of reducing costs. However, the real payback is this new level of agility and flexibility that provides fresh opportunities for businesses and their partners.

In essence, to get the biggest bang out of SOA, an organization needs to fundamentally change the way it makes IT investments. It must begin to coordinate even more with business partners to rationalize investments. It must also begin to break down some of those individual business project silos because they may be building redundant services. That lends to breaking down barriers of how projects are funded. Instead of funding them individually, a holistic model should be followed. This entails viewing these projects proactively and identifying those services that are already being built or have been built by another project and insisting on reuse. In the end, companies that embrace these concepts and new practices will come closest to reaching SOA nirvana.

Moore's Law has held true for decades. The semiconductor industry and IT shops that rely on distributed servers have become dependent on its continuation, and price per cycle remains one of the predominant methods of evaluating platforms. However, the commodity packaging technology that has been driving Moore's Law and has been so critical to semiconductor industry economics, is now reaching a technological

limit with respect to power density. As a result, processor frequency is becoming unreliable as the primary driver of capacity enhancements.

With this slowing of processor-level frequency growth, parallel chips/cores are emerging as the predominant path for future performance enhancement. Future improvements in server capacity will have to come from more efficient software and application designs that can account for this parallelism and treat dual hardware systems as a single logical entity. The semiconductor manufacturers have already begun the transition to these multi-core machines, but the software industry has not kept pace, relying instead on the growth of single processor/ thread performance. Once this growth path dries up, some profound changes will have to occur at the software level to address the inevitability of parallel processing.

This will not be a small task. Every aspect of software design, work-load management, security policies and transactional integrity, to name some important ones, will have to be overhauled to account for the fact that an application that used to be able to run on a single thread now may be forced to run across multiple threads. More importantly, these changes will have to occur at the underlying operating system and middleware layers so that the "application programming" model remains unchanged and existing business systems can be carried forward without modification.

This is not the first time the computing industry has undergone such a major change. In the 1980s, water-cooled mainframe technology

It is prudent to roll out SOA at a pace that makes good business sense, but **» SOA SECRET** it is equally wise to do so within the context of an enterprise-wide road map that plots where the organization wants to go and what infrastructure investments are required.

> ## THE TRUE SECRET OF SOA SUCCESS IS TO EMBRACE SOA WITH A VIEW TOWARDS THE GOALS OF THE ENTERPRISE AND CAPITALIZE ON THE BENEFITS OF A CENTRALIZED DEPLOYMENT APPROACH. 🟥

reached the limit of Moore's Law and faced a similar challenge. Mainframe hardware was reconfigured with parallel processors and its operating system and middleware were redesigned to support a tightly coupled cluster model to drive both scale and availability. All system policies and practices were re-engineered for this parallel deployment model without disruption to the existing programming model. Applications were insulated from this radical shift in the underlying processor structure.

Today's mainframe has solved the technological issues that the distributed server industry is just beginning to grapple with. Along the way, all of the critical software necessary for realizing the promises of SOA has been seamlessly added to these new parallel mainframes. The service-oriented IT that is "re-discovering" the inherent value of adopting a more centralized approach to SOA deployment will find this new breed of centralized servers to be indispensable.

THE SECRET OF SOA

When considering deployment options, an enterprise is faced with two fundamental choices:

1. Consolidate to a small number of large parallel systems, or
2. Distribute to a large number of small parallel systems

Each choice has its technological advantages and disadvantages, each of which will be discussed at length in later chapters of this book. For now, consider the following points:

» It is difficult to drive high levels of utilization in a massively distributed topology where each system is dedicated to a single type of
work. Low utilization drives the need to over-provision, thus
decreasing efficiency and responsiveness. Centralization tends to
require less unused capacity.

» Security is exposed every time a service must pass a machine
boundary. Reducing the number of wire hops will make security
easier to impose and manage.

» Software (and hardware, for that matter) will always need to be
upgraded and patched. No matter how much automation is brought
to bear, applying a patch to 1,000 servers introduces more business
risk than applying the same patch to a single server.

» It's smart to avoid single points of failure in both hardware and software, but the level of redundancy necessary is directly correlated to
the quality of the platform. Achieving business resilience with massively parallel deployment topologies carries its own type of business risk. Reducing the number of moving parts can actually
enhance business resilience.

» How easy is it to maintain the integrity of a transaction as it hops
from system to system? Is an end-to-end transaction auditable?
Does it comply with all appropriate mandates? Again, reducing the
number of wire hops will make it easier to ensure that data is not
corrupted.

» There is more to consider when distributing applications than mere
wire speed. Every time a machine boundary is crossed, a lot of work
must be done to first prepare the request to wire format and then
reconstitute in on the other end of the wire. A surprising amount of
processing power can be required.

Centralization of infrastructure does not contradict the decentralization
of services, nor does it hinder an incremental approach to SOA adoption. Services are simply abstractions of business processes. How
they are developed has no direct correlation to how they are physically

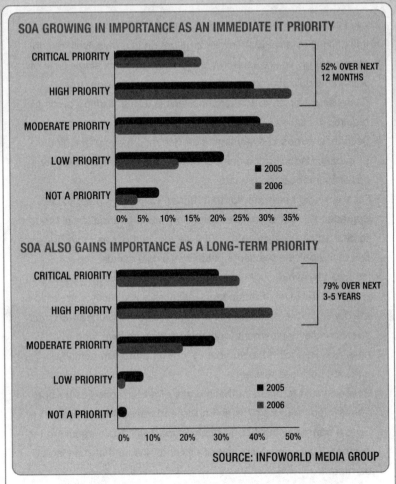

SOA GROWING IN IMPORTANCE AS AN IMMEDIATE IT PRIORITY

- CRITICAL PRIORITY
- HIGH PRIORITY

52% OVER NEXT 12 MONTHS

- MODERATE PRIORITY
- LOW PRIORITY
- NOT A PRIORITY

■ 2005
■ 2006

0% 5% 10% 15% 20% 25% 30% 35%

SOA ALSO GAINS IMPORTANCE AS A LONG-TERM PRIORITY

- CRITICAL PRIORITY
- HIGH PRIORITY

79% OVER NEXT 3-5 YEARS

- MODERATE PRIORITY
- LOW PRIORITY
- NOT A PRIORITY

■ 2005
■ 2006

0% 10% 20% 30% 40% 50%

SOURCE: INFOWORLD MEDIA GROUP

deployed. A large enterprise will likely have hundreds of services in support of its various organizations. Each service can be deployed on its own isolated infrastructure domain, or all services can be consolidated to a more centralized and manageable deployment domain. Either way, the business flexibility of SOA is retained. The question then becomes: Which model provides a greater degree of efficiency and governance?

It is prudent to roll out SOA at a pace that makes good business sense, but it is equally wise to do so within the context of an

enterprise-wide road map that plots where the organization wants to go and what infrastructure investments are required. Enterprises that struggle with SOA deployments are most often those that focus their SOA efforts on one small piece of the business at a time. They fund a pilot project the traditional way, expecting a cost/benefit payback for that project alone, without considering the overall enterprise context. If that project works, they proceed with a second and then a third in a similar fashion. In the end, they are left with an unwieldy mess of isolated, inefficient and unmanageable deployment domains. Remember what Gartner said about the importance of governance to midsize-to-large projects? It is far easier to govern a few things than a lot of things. Enterprises that are most successful in deploying SOA also tend to take an incremental approach, but always within the context of a broader, enterprise-wide plan. They do not try and justify the return on investment at the project level alone.

Conventional wisdom states that SOA deployment considerations are immaterial and that the main concern is the development model and how applications are built. SOA applications can be developed on a wide variety of platforms, which is a good thing because it allows developers to build their services within a comfort zone of familiar technology. But this flexibility also creates a natural inertia to deploy the applications to the same, familiar technology. Often, this technology choice is defended on the basis of cost efficiency (for the application, not the enterprise) and a "good enough" level of quality (again, for the application).

This view is shortsighted. It does not accept SOA as a disruptive technology. Not making the necessary changes to an IT organization that optimizes an SOA deployment is a dangerous game that can put the enterprise in a position of facing a greater than acceptable risk. It could result in both a considerable amount of future difficulty and reduction of the business advantages to be gained by consolidating infrastructure. As Forrester Group states: "To evolve to an SOA plat-

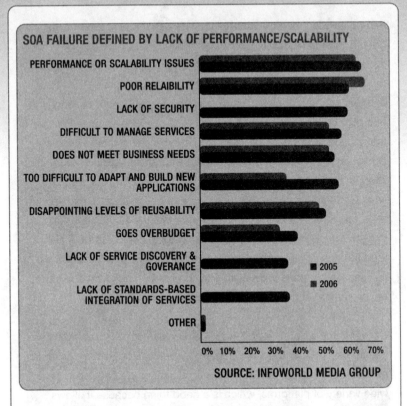

SOA FAILURE DEFINED BY LACK OF PERFORMANCE/SCALABILITY

SOURCE: INFOWORLD MEDIA GROUP

form that supports the big impact potential of responsive, adaptive, continually optimized business, you must get the architecture right."[6]

Yankee Group has pointed out that "there is a great deal of waste when each application is supported by its own discrete infrastructure stack ... the result is escalating costs, too many products and vendors (and associated licenses and terms), long lead times for customized application development and rigid IT functionality that often misses the mark of mapping to a business's changing goals and needs. Data and intellectual property are scattered within myriad repositories and within applications, making the exercise of this intelligence spotty and dependent on manual processes with little automation. Instead of being a catalyst to business transformation, IT has too often been a source of inertia for any change."[7]

SOA is a disruptive technology that requires a bold new approach towards information technology deployment. Deployment of business services is a critical consideration, one not to be taken lightly. The true secret of SOA success is to embrace SOA with a view towards the goals of the enterprise and capitalize on the benefits of a centralized deployment approach.

Paul DiMarzio is an SOA strategist at IBM, as well as a consulting software product design professional with IBM System z Software and On Demand Business Strategy Manager.

Since 2003 he has worked in the IBM System z software brand organization developing and maintaining an overall z/OS on-demand business technical strategy, focusing on SOA. The author joined IBM in 1984 as an MVS developer and has been involved with S/390-System z operating system and middleware software for most of his career, working in both IBM's Systems and Technology Group and Software Group. In addition to his current strategic responsibilities, he evangelizes the value of z/OS as a deployment platform for SOA middleware, in particular IBM's WebSphere software offerings.

1 Forrester Trends: SOA Will Change How IT Works, by Alex Cullen, May 31, 2005.
2 Aberdeen Group, The SOA in IT Benchmark Report: What CIOs Should Know About How SOA is Changing IT, December 2005.
3 Computerworld, American Modern Pioneers SOA in Infrastructure Overhaul, by Steve Ulfelder, March 13, 2006.
4 Gartner Group, Gartner Research, Management Update: Predicts 2006: The Strategic Impact of SOA Broadens, by Jess Thompson et al, November 23, 2005.
5 Forrester Topic Overview: Service-Oriented Architecture, by Randy Heffner, December 22, 2005.
6 Forrester, Your Strategic SOA Platform Vision, by Randy Heffner, March 29, 2005.
7 Yankee Group, DecisionNote Overview: SOA Closes the Gap Between Technology Benefits and Business Requirements, by Dana Gardner, March 14, 2005.

Chapter

2

THE SOA INFORMATION MANUFACTURING SYSTEM

To best understand service-oriented architecture's potential impact on business functions, it's important to 'get' why SOA isn't just another IT initiative. In doing so, IT has a greater chance of changing its reputation as a profit-drainer into one the rest of the company truly appreciates.

BY TERRY KEENE

Every year, *CIO* magazine conducts a nationwide survey of top IT management. Every year, this survey shows the No. 1 priority is aligning IT strategies with business objectives. Obviously, if the problem had been solved, it wouldn't continue to be the top issue. But there's been a change at the top. For the first time, this year CIOs said that their No. 1 priority is to help drive revenue growth.

It's about time. Traditionally, IT has always been considered a cost center despite proof the investments have also yielded profits of a different sort. Service-oriented architecture now provides a new taxonomy with which to base agreement with management on the value of IT. In its rawest form, SOA is the concept of designing business processes as services and then deploying IT infrastructure specifically to support those identified services. It also provides a means to discuss the position and value of IT within the business infrastructure with business managers. In essence, the business process and the IT structure to support that process are encapsulated into

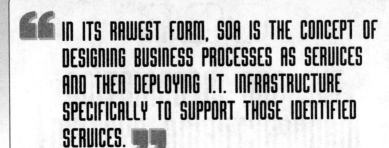

> IN ITS RAWEST FORM, SOA IS THE CONCEPT OF DESIGNING BUSINESS PROCESSES AS SERVICES AND THEN DEPLOYING I.T. INFRASTRUCTURE SPECIFICALLY TO SUPPORT THOSE IDENTIFIED SERVICES.

something called a service, and that service is being published for the world to see and use.

SOA ORIGINS

Software reuse is often highlighted as an important SOA benefit. That idea originated from a software development discipline called object-oriented design. This moved software developers away from viewing applications as integrated lines of code to architecting software to look like real life, with real problems, processes, people and businesses called objects. The real key to object orientation was in the design philosophy of the software. In turn, the biggest challenge was software developers now viewing problems in terms of objects that are part of everyday life. In essence, they now designed their programs the way the world works. This idea of writing and publishing an object, with its own methods and its own attributes, helped create the concept of reuse. Methods and attributes could be "inherited" by other similar objects to shorten the development cycle. This was a novel idea and one of the important values that emerged from object orientation. It resulted in dramatically reducing the cost and effort of writing new code.

Object orientation may have been one important enabler of SOA. A second was developing the means to communicate with, and between, those objects. If an object is published and somebody wants to use it, the person needs to be able to find it, determine what it does, attach to it, use it and then detach from it. This entire process also had to be accomplished with an acceptable level of security. An open industry standard, the Common Object Request Brokering Architecture (CORBA), was developed to accomplish just that. Microsoft also developed an approach to provide this same functionality, COM and DCOM, but strictly for Microsoft products. However, no standards of interoperability between Microsoft's products and CORBA were developed, drastically inhibiting the impact and general acceptance of object-orientated software development.

SOA is actually the confluence of three separate technologies: object orientation; the general acceptance of open system standards; and the World Wide Web and the attendant web browser user interface. Much of what is currently happening within IT is a natural process called open systems.

WHAT IS 'OPEN SYSTEMS'?

The truth is that the definition of open systems has nothing to do with computing. Open systems is a market dynamic. Every major commodity industry in the world is an open system or it never achieves commodity status. If an industry can't get to open systems, then it's deemed a niche market and will probably be replaced at some point by another niche market. Open systems is a major step in the maturation of an industry. There is a four-step process to achieving open systems:

1. A product has massive appeal.
2. Standards are set around that product and everybody agrees to those standards.

> **» SOA SECRET**
>
> The real key to object orientation was in the design philosophy of the software. In turn, the biggest challenge was software developers now viewing problems in terms of objects that are part of everyday life. In essence, they now designed their programs the way the world works.

3. Everyone must have access to those standards to enter the market. This is fundamental to the concept.
4. Through adoption, a mass commodity market builds and matures.

Industry after industry has grown through these four steps. But not the computer industry. The problem is standards: No one seems to agree on them, and that's because Microsoft, which currently has the lion's share of the market in many areas, refuses to make its standards available. Therefore, the industry can't get beyond Step 2.

There are two ways to set standards. One's by committee; for example, there's the Open Source Organization that is setting the standards for the whole open source movement. The other's by volume. That is how Microsoft sets standards. The critical point is that in order to move the IT industry into an open systems industry, standards must be agreed upon and everybody must be allowed to use them. The reason that Linux has been so influential is because, for the first time, it has raised a challenge to Microsoft. In response to that challenge, Microsoft has been forced to do some things differently. Linux's growing popularity meant the No. 1 player had to capitulate to open systems.

Still, the major force to open systems adoption came from the Internet. Suddenly, there were standards for Internet communications that the entire world accepted, and Microsoft had nothing to do with them. Standards like HTTP, HTML, even XML, as well as a standard browser—all of these caused Microsoft to adopt someone else's standards for the first time. The problem remains that true open systems are impossible without Microsoft, because it still owns such a huge portion of computing markets. Many in the industry hope that Linux's rise will encourage the software giant to finally change its tune.

Another set of standards, called web services, has unfolded as part of this open source concept, which plays with these Internet standards and include UDDI, WSDL and SOAP. These standards created the ability for little objects to be created that were able to exist on the Web and register themselves. Security standards are currently being developed for point-to-point protected connections between objects. Through open standards, object-oriented applications can be used and reused.

In essence, open systems in computers would mean that:
» Every application would work on every computer
» Every application would look the same on every computer
» Every application would work the same on every computer
» A computer can be bought from any vendor

Hence, open systems in computing are all about the application—not the hardware, the operating system, the database or object request broker. By combining three technologies — 1) object orientation and object-based design; 2) web services or standard connectivity to those objects; and 3) the Internet or a standard interface — global access to any object could exist. This is the core underlying technology enabling service-oriented architecture.

I.T. AS INFORMATION MANUFACTURING SYSTEMS

Business is more and more about data, and at its core IT is about Information Manufacturing Systems. It takes a raw material called data; puts that material into a manufacturing process called applications and middleware; and out the other end comes finished goods called information. This information is distributed to customers

Industry after industry has grown through four distinct steps. But not the » **SOA SECRET** computer industry. The problem is standards: no one seems to agree on them, and that's because Microsoft, which currently has the lion's share of the market in many areas, refuses to make its standards available. Therefore, the industry can't get beyond Step 2.

MUCH OF WHAT IS CURRENTLY HAPPENING WITHIN I.T. IS A NATURAL PROCESS CALLED OPEN SYSTEMS. "

through networks, internets, LANs, metro-networks, etc. That product must be delivered to customers when they need it, where they need it, in a form they can use and at a price that they can afford. IT is now part of the business infrastructure.

With a commitment to SOA, the IT organization is suddenly manufacturing a product, information, specifically to support a business process and publish it as a service. SOA can enable an organization to work not only internally but to connect to its critical suppliers, important customers and even to competitors. So now an application can be published that is matched up with a business process that people can access and use. The security, of course, must be in place so unauthorized people don't have the authority to use it.

Consider the fact that a service is actually an object written for a specific business process. The concept of object-orientated programs aligned with business processes constitutes a service that ultimately defines SOA. The beauty of that name is all about branding and brand recognition. SOA can be that brand that is instantly recognized by business executives, business managers, business consultants and the business press.

The concept of SOA is simple. It identifies a business process; IT creates an object to support that business process. The objects themselves are self-contained and have their own attributes and methods. It is also self-sustaining, self-managing, self-controlling and knows what to do. It can take orders and execute them based on the data and its attributes. Marry that with a business process;

write an object to support that process; and—*presto!*—a service is created. This service provides the capability to execute a business process. Of equal importance, modifications to both the object and the process are simple and easy to do. This is where payback begins. Once an object is written, along with its error code management and test routines, it can be modified and tested without rewriting these codes and procedures.

In addition, once written, an object is autonomous and can connect to anything. The value of that autonomy is that other objects can be plugged into it at will as long as they match up with the methods and the attributes of that particular object. Other objects can then be plugged into this combined object to create a chain. These chains are not easy to write. But the beauty is that they only have to be developed once and then they can be shared. So, as sharing of these fundamental objects becomes common, an inventory of service modules will be created that allow IT to move in almost any direction very quickly and at a much lower cost. That is where ROI is achieved.

CHOOSING AN ARCHITECTURE

The question now becomes how to choose architecture to make all of this happen. What is the decision point? What are the criteria? Here is an illustration.

A grocery chain needs to haul perishable goods to its stores from the warehouse every day. Its current need is to purchase new refrigeration

By combining three technologies — 1) object orientation and object-based design; 2) web services or standard connectivity to those objects; and 3) the Internet or a standard interface — global access to any object could exist. This is the core underlying technology enabling service-oriented architecture.

» SOA SECRET

vans to make these daily deliveries. In deciding on refrigeration vans, the company's procurement team found the tractors to pull those refrigeration vans, but not by meeting with the vice president of transportation and the chief mechanic and the head of the parts organization. Nor did it look at every single tractor trailer, assess their dual rear tires, check the differential, lift the hood, look at the 12-cylinder, fuel-injected diesel engines and get up and shift 12 gears forward. No. The procurement guys called the tractor leasing companies and said, "Okay, we want to lease a good tractor. It has to be a cost-effective tractor and has to meet four criteria:

1. Will it do what we want?
2. Will it fit our budget?
3. Will it work 24 hours a day, seven days a week?
4. If it breaks, how fast can it be fixed?"

That is all a company also needs to know about its SOA IT architecture. The specific attributes of the system are irrelevant. It is about business.

Will it do what we want? Most technology can fulfill a company's needs. However, chances are that an organization is not going to use all, or even most, of the technology it buys. According to IBM studies conducted in hundreds of IT organizations, most distributed Intel servers running Windows operate at about 5% utilization. The big distributed servers, doing several applications, will grind at 15% to maybe 25%. If they push their limits much higher than 50%, the systems will most likely crash. On top of that, this system may reach peak capacity at some point, and when it comes close or surpasses that threshold, it will surely crash. Companies design their configurations to take into account this peak utilization. Hence, they are going to have more system capacity than they can use. Or they are going to have to choose more efficient centralized servers that are able to handle more than one task efficiently. That's the land of the mainframe.

Will it fit our budget? Most companies do not consider all the costs associated with an IT infrastructure. They typically look only at the hardware, software and maintenance costs. Those are tangible and come out of the capital budget. The costs that get less attention are human resource costs, which tend to absorb the greatest amount of funds, by far. People costs include system implementation, integration and daily maintenance, support, caring and feeding. With open systems, remember, every application runs on every computer, from any vendor, "out of the box," thus greatly reducing these costs.

As a company adds servers, the amount of people it takes to support or maintain them grows linearly. Unfortunately, those costs do not hit the capital budget so they are not quite as visible to the company. Hence, the question "Will it fit our budget?" is broader than the combined unit cost of hardware and software. Obviously, if a company buys a $3,000 two-way Intel server, that unit cost is going to be lower than a $50,000 four-way UNIX box or a $1 million one-way mainframe. The unit cost for hardware and, usually, software is always going to be lower for smaller, cheaper boxes. However, a true assessment should measure all costs. For example, the cost of managing mainframe systems has dropped over the last 10 years in tandem with its exponential increase in performance. That is because IBM keeps enhancing the performance, and the number of people it takes to maintain those servers has gone down because of more automated processes.

> **SOA SECRET**
>
> Companies still believe that the unit cost for mainframes is too high. The important point being missed in that assessment is that with SOA, IT becomes a mission-critical part of the business infrastructure. As such, it cannot afford to be down. The mainframe is so much better at mission-critical applications because it has built-in hardware, software, system and network reliability and redundancy. In every other environment this has to be built in by the user.

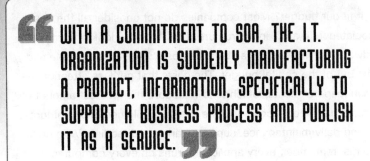

> **WITH A COMMITMENT TO SOA, THE I.T. ORGANIZATION IS SUDDENLY MANUFACTURING A PRODUCT, INFORMATION, SPECIFICALLY TO SUPPORT A BUSINESS PROCESS AND PUBLISH IT AS A SERVICE.**

Will it work 7 days a week, 24 hours a day, 365 days a year? A company can get a system to work; the important question is: Will it work 7 days a week, 24 hours a day? Consider that IT is now morphing from a cost center to a services provider business center. With SOA done right, services are built that everybody in the enterprise can access and utilize whenever, and wherever, they want to. The emergence of individual mobility means this access can be done from Blackberries, Treos or other mobile devices worldwide. If IT is going to be a viable part of an enterprise, it can't afford to be down.

The classic reliability figures for a Windows Server or UNIX box comes in at the range of 98.5% to 99.9%. Sounds good, except 99.9% still means a lot of minutes of down time in a 24/7/365 world. UNIX systems could be made 99.999% reliable, but it would take many systems and many people to accomplish. This level of reliability has been built into the mainframe over the course of 50 years. IBM mainframe developers are obsessed with 99.999%, even the theoretically unachievable 100% reliability. Also, with a mainframe, there is only one "throat to choke." If it breaks, they get it fixed, quickly. There are no finger pointing or hardware/software/middleware boundaries to navigate. IBM does it all. After all, the last critical question is, *"If it breaks, how fast can you get it fixed?"* Repair by committee is never an efficient option.

Companies still believe that the unit cost for mainframes is too high. The important point being missed in that assessment is that with SOA, IT becomes a mission-critical part of the business infrastructure. As such, it cannot afford to be down. The mainframe is so much better at mission-critical applications because it has built-in hardware, software, system and network reliability and redundancy. In every other environment this has to be built in by the user.

PROTECTING THE TRUE ASSETS: DATA

Every service deployed as part of SOA involves a mission-critical application working 24 hours a day, 7 days a week. Even more critically, that service attaches to, and interfaces with, data. Data is IT's raw material and needs to be accurate, protected, managed, maintained and recoverable. A company needs to ensure its integrity, security and availability, as well as its privacy, so that authorized users have access while the unauthorized are barred. Services can be deployed anywhere, but not data.

Right now, the handling of data is analogous to the days of stuffing currency under mattresses or burying it in backyards. Every company owns, maintains and supports its own data. Even within a single company, each line of business often owns its view of the corporate data. Therefore, there is a large amount of replication. Personal information exists in literally thousands of places. Typically, when individuals go to the credit bureaus for a credit analysis, for instance, there are three

The challenge that IT departments are going to have in making the shift to » **SOA SECRET** SOA is to become intimately involved in the business process. Once IT accepts this mind shift, it will become obvious how critical these services are to the company. Hence, developing infrastructure to support those services will be even more important than anything IT has put together to date.

 MOST TECHNOLOGY CAN FULFILL A COMPANY'S NEEDS. HOWEVER, CHANCES ARE THAT AN ORGANIZATION IS NOT GOING TO USE ALL, OR EVEN MOST, OF THE TECHNOLOGY IT BUYS.

different views of their data that, for the most part, do not agree with the real situation. The same holds for key business information on customers, inventory and trade. Exacerbating this situation is a general propensity to decentralize data, in essence to distribute it among divisions and even remote locations. When data is distributed, it must be replicated. The minute it's replicated, it's no longer accurate because replicated versions can be changed without impacting the original data. If data were stored only in a central repository it would remain consistently accurate and be protected and secure.

The ideal solution for data would be very large, accurate and reliable boxes. A great example is the IBM mainframe or IBM P-series AIX, which is very much like the mainframe in some respects. Even large HP systems that can scale up to accommodate large amounts of data and have a large processing capacity will suffice. Theoretically those are the ideal places to put data. However, centralized data must reside in a place that is absolutely secure, reliable, available, protected and quickly recovered. Because centralized data must service many different requirements simultaneously and rapidly, the ideal solution in a perfect world would be to put all data on a mainframe and all services on a reliable infrastructure. Many companies think that UNIX and Windows are low-cost application solutions; however, the inefficiencies of those environments has already been discussed. If a company owns a mainframe, most applications can execute in that environment if SOA applications are deployed. The mainframe has implemented Java, Web-based and Linux applications native on the architecture. A

Windows environment is not the ideal solution. There are just some things that Windows cannot do.

Extending the concept of IT as a manufacturer, in every industry the ideal solution would be to manufacture and distribute product from a central location. One location is less expensive, takes less infrastructure, fewer employees and management to operate. And it has much better control over accuracy, reliability and security. If it were possible for Ford Motors to manufacture every car from Dearborn, Michigan, it would do so. It doesn't because it can't maintain customer satisfaction with that business model. It can't ship cars at the speed of light. The IT business, in sharp contrast, can. The problem is that IT doesn't view itself as a manufacturer. However, if IT wants to play in the business world, it must view itself differently. Consider that what IT is doing is manufacturing information. In that regard, doing it from a central location is the optimal solution.

MAKING IT CRITICAL TO BUSINESS

SOA is about encapsulating business processes with IT to support those processes as unique services. This has created a juncture at which business and IT are being forced together. The challenge that IT departments are going to have in making the shift to SOA is to become intimately involved in the business process. Once IT accepts this mind shift, it will become obvious how critical these services are to the company. Hence, developing infrastructure to support those services will be even more important than anything IT has put together to date. Because, up to now, IT has been able to separate the data, the application, the middleware, the network, the transmission, the inter-process communications and the messaging from each other, deploy them almost independently and then spend a huge amount of time integrating them back together.

When organizations start encapsulating business processes with IT, much of the result is in the form of basic business applications, many

accessed on handheld systems. These applications will do inventory, shipping, receiving, picking and packing in the warehouse. Some will be on a delivery truck, others in a manager's office on the top floor of a glassed-in room looking out over a manufacturing plant. They will be everywhere within a business operation. That is the beauty of SOA. A user can go out and get a service, run it, get another service, run it, and put them together to do what they need to do, get the needed data to create the information and get rid of it all on a small mobile device.

As this migration from a technology-based information world to a business-process based information world continues, it is critical that the supporting systems have the highest level of reliability, availability, security, serviceability, redundancy and recoverability. The grocery delivery truck sitting on the road with perishable goods and a 45-minute deadline will depend on this process to provide the address, location, directions, destination, invoice for signature and packing list updated accurately-and within minutes. If not, the product is worthless.

The result of this SOA approach is 100% reliant on the system's ability to deliver it where it is needed, when it is needed, with the information that is needed and at a price that the customer is willing to pay. Everything that IT has been paid to do over all these years in creating and enhancing reliability, availability, security, serviceability, redundancy and recoverability is going to be more critical than it has ever been. Choose your partners wisely.

Terry Keene is president of Integration Systems, LLC, which has provided consulting services to more than 1,000 corporations and organizations globally in almost every industry. Prior to beginning his consulting career, he established one of the first systems integration firms that specialized in commercial UNIX implementations, and as an independent software vendor he developed MenuMagic, a complete system management software application for the UNIX environment. Keene graduated from the U.S. Military Academy at West Point and received a master's degree in electrical engineering from the Georgia Institute of Technology, where he later taught computer engineering and design as an adjunct professor.

Chapter

⬜⬜③⬜⬜

MAKING SOFTWARE REUSE A REALITY

One of the core benefits of service-oriented architecture is that it may provide a means to achieve one of the holy grails of IT shops everywhere – software reuse. While simple in concept and with obvious advantages, the reuse of various pieces of software is not often standard operating policy. This chapter discusses difficulties inherent in software reuse and how they might be overcome.

BY WILLIAM BUCKINGHAM

Service-oriented architecture promises a range of benefits to organizations, but perhaps none is sought more than the ability to reuse software. Chief among the tangible benefits is *money*.

A commitment to reuse has an impact on the cost of both application development and maintenance.

One noted industry expert, Martin Griss, broke it down in a 1993 IBM Systems Journal article: "It appears that product development costs, factoring in the cost of producing, supporting and integrating reusable software components, can decrease by a sustainable 10% to 12%; defect rates in delivered products can drop drastically to 10% of their former levels; and long-term maintenance costs can drop from 20% to 50% of their former values when several products share the same, high-quality components."[1]

 SOFTWARE REUSE IS ESPECIALLY VALUABLE NOW SINCE SO MANY INDUSTRIES ARE MULTI-CHANNEL IN NATURE. "

Much of the important thinking on software reuse was produced in the mid-1990s, before the term service-oriented architecture was coined. The degree to which benefits are realized within a company varies widely by source. The following table provides a sample of the range of opinion.

SAMPLE OPINIONS ON SOFTWARE REUSE

FACTOR	REPORTED BENEFITS
Development	» **Martin Griss:** "Reduce software development costs by 10% to 15%"[2] » **Emmett Paige Jr.:** "Overall software development cost: reduction of around 15%, to as much as 75%, for long-term projects (this includes the overhead cost of developing reusable assets and supporting their use)"[3] » **Gartner Group** estimates that consistent reuse methodology increases application development productivity by 30%. It is reasonable to predict that a reuse program that includes all required elements will produce an ongoing annual ROI equal to or greater than 200% within two years for a shop with 100 developers.[4] » **Analyst Richard Hunter:** "10% to 20%"[5]

FACTOR	REPORTED BENEFITS
Maintenance	» **Griss:** "Reduce the maintenance costs by 2 to 5 times"[6] » **Paige:** "Maintenance cost: reductions of 5 to 10 times"[7] » **Various authors:** "Long-term maintenance costs can drop from 20% to 50% of their former values when several products share the same, high-quality components"[8]
Time-to-market	» **Griss:** "Reduce the time to market for a product by 1 1/2 to 2 times"[9] » **Paige:** "Time to market reductions of 2 to 5 times"[10] » **Various authors:** "25% reduced time to repair"[11] » **Academics:** "25% reduced Schedule"[12] » **Academics:** "50% reductions in integration time"[13]
Quality	» **Academics:** "20% reduction in customer complaints"[14] » **Academics:** "20% to 35% improvement in quality"[15] » **Academics:** "Defect density: reductions from 5 to 10 times"[16] » **Various authors:** "Effect rates in delivered products can drop drastically to 10% of their former levels"[17]

Software reuse is not free. Industry estimates indicate it costs 60% more » **SOA SECRET**
to develop a reusable component than it does for one
meant for a single use, according to the 1997 book
Measuring Software Reuse by Jeffrey S. Poulin.

FACTOR	REPORTED BENEFITS
Training	» **Academics:** "20% reduction in training costs"[18] General » **Academics:** "14% to 68% increase in productivity"[19] » **Academics:** "400% return on investment"[20] » **Academics:** "Organizations have realized reuse benefits, such as 900% productivity increases, cycle-time reductions of 70% and cost reductions of 84%"[21]

The potential reduction in development costs range from 10% to 75%. Factors impacting this reduction include:

» The industry
» The type of software being developed
» The number of possible instances of reuse
» The effective lifespan of the reusable software
» Development technologies and their evolution

The reduction in maintenance costs can be even greater. Consider the following example. A bank develops three programs to calculate interest rates on loans: one for call center staff; one for use over the Internet; and one for the branch offices. If a governance or legislative change occurs that forces this bank to incorporate new risk factors when they calculate a loan, the effort to implement this change must be made three times. However, if one piece of reusable software had been developed and the three loan processing systems in each of the delivery channels all share it, maintenance only is made once, reducing implementation costs by two-thirds, or 67%.

There also are intangible benefits to consider. Software reuse is especially valuable now since so many industries are multi-channel in nature. In the retail environment, a store might sell the same product at

a store front, via a catalogue or through a web site. While prices might vary across these channels, they need to be driven by a central pricing policy and fed from the same source.

A business needs to provide customers with both a consistent experience and consistent results. Being consistent leads to higher customer satisfaction and avoids potential embarrassment. For instance, if a company is reusing the same loan calculation component, there is only one authoritative place for the system to go to calculate loans. Having one source for the calculation ensures consistency. Without consistency, the overall quality of service is in question.

Going back to our hypothetical bank, say it has three different loan processing systems: one for the Internet; one for the branch; and another for the call center. A customer decides he needs a car loan. First, he contacts the call center. The agent offers him an interest rate of x percent. He feels he can afford that arrangement. That night, the client goes online to double check the numbers. He discovers that the interest rate is x *minus* 1/2 percent and he is happier, still. The next day while downtown, he decides to close the deal in person. He walks into a branch, finds a loan officer and inquires about the same loan. The banker offers him an interest rate of x *plus* 1/2 percent! Needless to say, the impact on this customer is likely to be negative and may cost the bank the customer's business.

THE COSTS OF SOFTWARE REUSE

Of course, software reuse is not free. An industry expert on the topic, Dr. Jeffrey Poulin, estimates it costs 60% more to develop a reusable component than it does for one meant for a single use.[22] A number of factors increase this cost. First, there are infrastructure investments. These might include the acquisition of new design and development technologies, such as new run-time environments like application servers, business process management (BPM) engines, an enterprise service bus (ESB) and some form of run-time monitoring technology. It

also takes time and effort to design a reusable component since a broader set of requirements might have to be considered. These requirements might be both on the business side (a broader set of situations the component might be used in) or technical in nature (higher levels of quality-of-service, a broader set of security requirements, etc.). More exhaustive and imaginative testing is usually required to ensure the component will work in all potential situations. A more mature look at quality assurance, raising it to the level of of an "engineering discipline," might be needed.

Even if the ideal component has been developed and is waiting to be used, there is still a cost associated with its exploitation. In most cases, potential consumers of a reusable service must define their requirements and ensure there is a match with an existing reusable component. The aforementioned Dr. Poulin estimates the effort to consume an existing piece of reusable software is only 20% of what it would cost to develop from scratch. Assume the aforementioned bank has four application development projects to build systems to satisfy similar requirements. The architects have seen potential overlap and specified that a common service be developed. The following cost model might justify this architectural position.

COST MODEL

	Base Cost	Adjustment for Reuse	Project Cost	Running Cost	Total Savings
Development Project	$100	Plus 60%	$160	$160	-$60
First instance of Reuse	$100	20% of Base Cost	$20	$180	-$20
Second instance of Reuse	$100	20% of Base Cost	$20	$200	$100
Third instance of Reuse	$100	20% of Base Cost	$20	$220	$180

Adopting stringent practices to ensure the development of reusable services may cost more in the short term, but it can provide substantial benefits over the long run. With the above model, the initial costs to build reusable services are higher, but the bank will break even as early as the third project.

The whole concept of costs and its allocation requires rethinking. To start, costs incurred through software reuse should not be thought of as an expense, but as an investment. Also, the internal responsibility for these costs must be reconsidered.

FAILURE - NOT THE PREFERRED OPTION

IT shops continue to build applications without regard to whether the targeted business problem has already been solved. Often, this is because the people developing solutions cannot find a reusable asset to leverage, or they simply believe their problem is so unique that no one has ever solved it.

Other reasons why companies do not successfully reuse application software are:
» Corporate culture
» Absence of a strategic platform
» No strategy or vision as to how they want to achieve software reuse
» A lack of understanding what assets they have that might be reused

Corporate culture is probably the most common reason for failure. For much of the history of IT, companies have encouraged the development of unique applications and discouraged using existing software. Twenty-year-old stories still circulate about employees being disci-

plined for plagiarism while trying to reuse existing software. Even in recent years, it has been acceptable for a business sponsor to block an opportunity to share functionality because the potential user's sponsor didn't help pay for it.

Why Do Companies Fail at SOA?

There is a perception by some in the IT industry that SOA equates to web services and vice versa. Some companies believe that if they enable a web-service interface (SOAP over HTTP), they have achieved "SOA." This simply is not true. While SOA can be delivered using web services, a set of incoherent web-service interfaces can also be delivered that have nothing in common and would not be considered SOA. This state has been referred to as *service-oriented chaos*, where any reuse of these interfaces is pure serendipity.

The truth is, SOA can be delivered using technologies other than web services. For example, many companies still run systems developed 20 to 30 years ago that are good examples of SOA. They use transaction processing technologies like IMS and CICS, message-oriented middleware like MQSeries or message brokers like MQSeries Integrator.

CREATING AN ENVIRONMENT FOR SOFTWARE REUSE

While the value in reusing software is clear, companies' perception of what software is and how it needs to be developed and managed is not. Many of the problems, sadly, are people problems that must be handled on an individual basis. After all, people can change, or people can be changed. Other problems, such as culture, knowledge management and software development practices are more commonplace.

Creating a Cultural Shift

Creating a development culture and environment that is conducive to software reuse is a key consideration in implementing SOA. Sometimes it might be as simple as making reuse "cool." Executive support is often necessary. Senior staff speaking positively about soft-

ware reuse remind staff about its strategic perspective. In the past, reuse initiatives have often been attempted and have failed. Executive messages have to be positive to overcome the inevitable chorus of "Here we go again."

Incentive programs should be used extensively. Coffee cups and T-shirts are fine, but developers need the value of software reuse underscored. One company has gone as far as flying a director of an internal reuse program halfway around the world to do nothing more than present a trophy in a brief ceremony to enterprising development teams. That company is sending a message that reuse is important.

Knowledge Management: If You Can't Find It, You Can't Reuse It
Many shops do not bother to actively track business systems they have developed over time, preferring instead to focus on active projects. As such, most have no comprehensive inventory of their existing business systems. Tacit knowledge of system composition is also lost with every terminated individual, every retirement, every dismissal and every resignation. Therefore, it also is important that software be both labeled and cataloged at development time. Without proper cataloging and documentation, the composition and capability of business systems is lost.

Adopting approaches like application portfolio management and reuse registries can give IT shops the ability to improve their knowledge by understanding what they have available for exploitation.

SOA can be delivered using technologies other than web services. **» SOA SECRET**
For example, many companies still run systems developed 20 to 30 years ago that are good examples of SOA. They use transaction processing technologies like IMS and CICS, message-oriented middleware like MQSeries or message brokers like MQSeries Integrator.

> THE GOOD NEWS IS THAT BUSINESSES HAVE DONE A GREAT JOB OVER THE LAST DECADE OR SO IN FOCUSING ON PROJECT MANAGEMENT FRAMEWORKS THAT IMPLEMENT PROJECT LIFE CYCLES. THE BAD NEWS IS THAT THIS FOCUS HAS OFTEN COME AT THE EXPENSE OF OTHER LIFE CYCLES. 🙸

Software as Products - Not Projects

The good news is that businesses have done a great job over the last decade or so in focusing on project management frameworks that implement project life cycles. The bad news is that this focus has often come at the expense of other life cycles. Often, organizations equate the notion of "life cycle" with the "project life cycle." Systems development life cycles and system life cycles have been forgotten. One result is that many companies have forgotten that their IT shops build a business product. Although this product is usually not for sale, it is product integral to running the business. That bank, for example, could not launch a new type of mortgage without the software to back it up.

Software is built as the result of a project typically created to meet a specific and current business requirement. When this requirement is met, the project is considered complete and the software is implemented, often with little or no documentation that captures the essence of what it does. To enable software reuse, companies need to consider software as a product, something that goes on beyond the end of the project that has intrinsic value and, therefore, should be considered an asset.

Treating Software as an Asset

Following are dictionary definitions of the word legacy: An "inheritance, bequest, that has come from an ancestor or predecessor or the past."[23] "A bequeathed sum of money or article, a "tangible or intangible thing handed down by a predecessor."[24] This sounds like legacy is something valuable and worth having. Sadly, legacy systems have been much maligned in the IT world, where they are often equated with something negative that holds back progress.

This attitude towards legacy needs to be recast. A business's so-called legacy systems are the result of years of investment, hard dollars and much effort. They are an asset and have value. These systems are vital to the functioning of a business and are often one of the most immediate and complete expressions of how a business operates. Moving to any new approach in IT, such as the adoption of SOA, introduces a certain amount of business risk. Using existing core business functions to develop new business services can dramatically reduce risk. It ensures those existing functions can continue to be used in existing contexts.

The term asset denotes something with intrinsic value and measurable worth. It is a notion that is built into the way a business manages itself. Companies continually evaluate the value of their real estate, capital equipment and even their office supplies. But these same companies need to understand the value of software they currently own. Few have a clue as to the value of business software they have purchased and built over the years, even after investing millions of dollars. A company that buys a hundred desks will consider them as

> To enable software reuse, companies need to consider software as a product, something that goes on beyond the end of the project that has intrinsic value and, therefore, should be considered an asset.
>
> ◉ **SOA SECRET**

CORPORATE CULTURE IS PROBABLY THE MOST COMMON REASON FOR FAILURE.

assets. Those desks could be destroyed and the company would only have to purchase more desks. Rebuilding the software that runs the business is a much more difficult proposition.

Putting the A in SOA

The A in SOA stands for architecture. There is value in simply knowing one's business better through the act of developing service-oriented architecture. Developing an SOA results in an IT shop knowing what services the business needs to operate. Defining how the services are implemented is just the next logical step. Development of an SOA, though, takes vision and support. It is not something that happens at the end of the day when there is nothing else to do or as the happy by-product of a project. Resources have to be assigned and the costs treated as an investment.

The development of an SOA can be compared to designing a paint-by-numbers artwork, with steps such as selecting a canvas, determining what the final image will be, sketching out the black lines and putting the numbers into the shapes defined by those black lines to determine the shape's color.

But, "painting the shapes" isn't part of the development of the SOA. Projects come along and develop parts of the system according to SOA (paint one or more of the shapes) with the appropriate resources at their disposal (the paint). Different shapes are painted in different colors. Implementation of the various services might be on different platforms depending on their importance and requirements. The implementation of a particular service might also change over time and move up or down the technology stack.

Lifecycle Management of Software

An emerging trend in the IT industry is application portfolio management (APM). As mentioned earlier, APM includes the notion of a life cycle for application systems. A life cycle encompasses the stages that systems go through: development; the requisite maintenance activities; and, eventually, retirement. The notion of a life cycle is integral to positioning software as a product. Just like a system, the software components a company might reuse also have a life cycle.

Ideally, the life cycle of the systems and the life cycle of their constituent components are in sync; problems can arise if they are not. For example, people responsible for an enterprise's technology life cycle determine that a particular application is dated and should be retired. In the meantime, another group concludes that a particular component of this application has a lot of potential. It has been exploited by six different applications over time and there may be additional opportunities, indicating it should be enhanced and anointed as a truly reusable asset.

Companies must, therefore, be careful in determining who has the responsibility for retiring software built for reuse. The architect responsible for a particular business domain and, by extension, a particular SOA is best suited to define the retirement process. It is that person's responsibility to have the global view of this application system and identify the reusable components.

Moving to any new approach in IT, such as the adoption of SOA, **» SOA SECRET** introduces a certain amount of business risk. Using existing core business functions to develop new business services can dramatically reduce risk. It ensures those existing functions can continue to be used in existing contexts.

The Proper Platform Selection

Developing the functionality to deliver an SOA must be based on solid technology. If a software component is going to be "reusable," it has to give the companies that might reuse it a sense that it has staying power. Just as one would not want to build a house on a bed of sand, reusable software should be built on a solid foundation of both software and hardware. There has to be longevity.

Currently, every vendor seems to offer at least one product claiming to be the ultimate SOA solution. Customers, however, should be careful when they consider buying these products since some are not mature. Developing mission-critical business functionality on immature technologies can be risky.

Just because applications are developed according to SOA is no reason to compromise on key issues like performance, transaction handling and quality of service. Using technology an IT shop already knows and trusts provides some comfort that the new strategic functionality being developed will have staying power. In many cases, continuing to use the platforms that existing business systems were developed on may be the best way to implement an SOA strategy.

Another reason to deploy reusable SOA services on existing platforms: long-lasting business systems already reside there. Placing reusable services on these platforms puts them adjacent to existing business functionality that is often encapsulated as part of the new services. In addition, data also reside there.

COMMITMENT TO SOFTWARE REUSE THROUGH SOA

An IT shop might build the best technical systems possible, but if those systems don't meet business needs it is wasting money. After all, if the various components of a system are not usable, they certainly aren't reusable. SOA is a proven way to help ensure systems are applicable to the business.

AN IT SHOP MIGHT BUILD THE BEST TECHNICAL SYSTEMS POSSIBLE, BUT IF THOSE SYSTEMS DON'T MEET BUSINESS NEEDS I.T. IS WASTING MONEY.

Consider an architect defining an SOA for a particular business domain. If the business domain is banking, for example, there might be fundamental services that support a minimum functionality familiar to both bankers and customers. Services may include familiar business processes like opening an account, making deposits or withdrawals and transferring funds.

In this case, the architect would not be defining a service that calculates the weight-bearing capacity of an airliner or that plans the daily provisioning of a fast food restaurant. Those services would not be applicable to the basic business model of banking. The organization needs to ensure the services are being defined according to specific business architecture and meet those specific requirements. This can be done with some basic business modeling. In some industries, models like these are already available. Industry consortia often provide basic definitions of how a particular business should look. In other situations, companies like IBM sell models for specific industries. In essence, business should have a clear role in defining *what* services are built. IT, however, must be given the freedom to decide *how* the services are built.

The Enterprise and the Domain
SOA requires governance at the enterprise level. However, the definition of what services best express the requirements of a particular business is often best handled locally, at the domain level. In large organizations with multiple lines of business, it is important to have a

sense of which SOA and software reuse decisions apply to the enterprise — and which are better left to a specific domain.

There are two compelling reasons why more than one SOA domain in a corporation is a good strategy. First is expertise. A large, multi-service financial institution (like Citibank, ABN AMRO or RBC Financial Group) delivers a number of different types of products reflecting the diversity of the businesses they've acquired or merged. In corporations of this magnitude, it is inevitable that the people responsible for enterprise strategy might have a background in one of the lines of business, such as banking, but have no idea about others, like insurance or brokerage. It might be best, then, that development of an SOA for a particular business is left in the hands of someone that has domain-specific expertise.

The second reason: having distinct SOAs provides more clarity. An example is the concept of "account." In discount brokerage, an account may be a set of holdings. In insurance, it may reflect a policy. In banking, an account might be checking or savings. It would be counterproductive to attempt to bring these three diverse sets of requirements together to create one "account service."

This is not to say, however, that the delivery of SOA and software reuse should be left strictly in the hands of line-of-business domains. These points need to be considered prior to making this decision.

» Will there be the need for an enterprise-level reuse strategy that provides a certain level of principles, minimum standards and framework?

» Will there be business services provided for aspects common to all

---

Just because the functionality is not designed to be enterprise in scope, there's no reason not to place the functionality on enterprise-class systems.

» **SOA SECRET**

parts of the company, such as general ledger, HR or CRM, that can best be identified by part of the organization that crosses lines of business?

Finally, just because the functionality is not designed to be enterprise in scope, there's no reason not to place the functionality on enterprise-class systems.

Presented below is a proposed model of how to develop a coherent set of reuse domains for a large corporation with multiple lines of business.

A FEDERATED MODEL FOR SOA

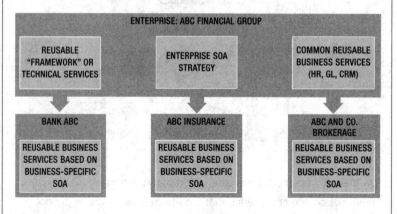

THE CARROT AND THE STICK: FUNDING AND GOVERNANCE

SOA governance is an important issue. A company may develop solid, reusable software with the best of intentions, but it is worthless if a junior programmer assigned to an important project decides he can do better than the SMEs that built the code he is meant to reuse. Architectural and managerial oversight is central to making software reuse happen. Commitment is necessary from the top.

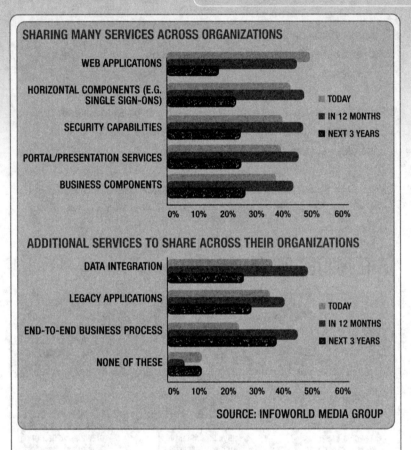

SHARING MANY SERVICES ACROSS ORGANIZATIONS

WEB APPLICATIONS
HORIZONTAL COMPONENTS (E.G. SINGLE SIGN-ONS)
SECURITY CAPABILITIES
PORTAL/PRESENTATION SERVICES
BUSINESS COMPONENTS

TODAY
IN 12 MONTHS
NEXT 3 YEARS

0% 10% 20% 30% 40% 50% 60%

ADDITIONAL SERVICES TO SHARE ACROSS THEIR ORGANIZATIONS

DATA INTEGRATION
LEGACY APPLICATIONS
END-TO-END BUSINESS PROCESS
NONE OF THESE

TODAY
IN 12 MONTHS
NEXT 3 YEARS

0% 10% 20% 30% 40% 50% 60%

SOURCE: INFOWORLD MEDIA GROUP

On the software production side, a company's commitment to SOA must include the acceptance that time-to-market concerns cannot always take precedence over software reuse. When software is built by a project team to address one particular business problem, the sponsors rarely think about whether they should provide funding to ensure software is reusable. On the contrary, building for reuse is often discouraged for fear the original builders may have to assume future maintenance and upgrade costs for all who use it. Not surprisingly, project managers are not always driven by the need to satisfy the common good; instead, they are far more focused on the calendar and meeting delivery dates.

One of the best ways to ensure they contribute to the development of reusable assets is through the budget process. To enable SOA and software reuse, companies need to consider new methods of funding software development. There are a number of different funding models to consider. Below are two suggestions.

Taxation Model
Organizational units are charged by a number of different formulas, such as the number or size of projects, assigned staff, etc. A majority of collected funds are allocated directly to infrastructure initiatives. Some of these funds, however, can be allocated to projects responsible for the development of reusable services.

Operational Charge-out
Organizational units are charged by utilization of reusable assets already in production. The charge must cover the resources used and include a premium to fund the maintenance of existing services and the development of new assets.

FINAL THOUGHT

For something to be reusable, it first has to be usable. Application functionality developed on platforms that have not stood the test of time is, of course, not very usable. Some systems, though, have been used for years. They were developed using technologies and platforms that not only survived, but thrived, in an evolving landscape of choices. These systems continue to provide a solid, proven foundation for the development of reusable assets.

William Buckingham has more than 25 years of experience on the IT side of the financial services industry. He has been both an applications programmer and software developer, involved in such things as data warehousing, check processing and automated teller machines.

In the mid-1990s, he became an IT architect at a time when it was not the most desired title to have on a business card. In 1997, he started asking the question "If we have all these application servers, what are the application services we are going to put on them?" In 1999 Gartner coined the term service-oriented architecture. In his current role, Buckingham is responsible for enabling software reuse throughout RBC Financial Group.

1   IBM Systems Journal: Software Reuse: From Library to Factory, by Martin L. Griss, 1993.

2   CrossTalk: Predictable Software: Order Out of Chaos, by Emmett Paige Jr., June 1994.

3   Software Reuse: Architecture, Process and Organization for Business Success, by Ivar Jacobsen, Martin Griss and Patrik Jonsson, 1997.

4   CIO Magazine: Once Is Not Enough, by Richard Hunter, March 1,1997.

5   IBM Systems Journal: Software Reuse: From Library to Factory, by Martin L. Griss, 1993.

6   CrossTalk: Predictable Software: Order Out of Chaos, by Emmett Paige Jr., June 1994.

7   Software Reuse: Architecture, Process and Organization for Business Success, by Ivar Jacobsen, Martin Griss and Patrik Jonsson, 1997.

8   Software Reuse: From Library to Factory, by Martin L. Griss, 1993.

9   Predictable Software: Order Out of Chaos, by Emmett Paige Jr., June 1994.

10 Software Reuse: Architecture, Process and Organization for Business Success , 1997.

11 Proceedings of the 2nd Annual West Virginia Reuse Education and Training Workshop: Management-Level Training, Oct. 25-27, 1993.

12 Ibid,

13 Ibid.

14 Ibid.

15 Ibid.

16 Software Reuse: Architecture, Process and Organization for Business Success , 1997

17 IBM Systems Journal: Software Reuse: From Library to Factory, by Martin L. Griss, 1993.

18 West Virginia Reuse Education and Training Workshop, 1993.

19 Ibid.

20 Ibid.

21 Independent Research Study of Software Reuse: Software Reuse: Because the Waters are Rising, by Eric Aranow, September 1994.

22 Measuring Software Reuse, by Jeffrey S. Poulin, 1997.

23 The Merriam-Webster Dictionary, 1974 edition.

24 The Shorter Oxford English Dictionary, fifth edition, 2002.

Chapter

◯◯④◯◯

THE ENTERPRISE VIEW OF BUSINESS PROCESS SERVING

The interdependency of many applications provides challenges for companies willing to adopt service-oriented architecture. Yes, it can be tough, but the benefits are well worth it if it's done properly.

BY TERRY BORDEN & BILL MITLEHNER

The functions and services a business performs in response to its customers generally break down into a collection of tasks. Some of these tasks may be automated, some done manually. But all need to be completed in a particular order to create a final result.

The order in which these tasks are organized, along with the guidelines around how they are completed, define the process. Typically, many of these tasks will overlap with others across the company duplicating efforts and potentially producing inconsistent results. This task duplication in software creation can cause multiple development and maintenance streams resulting in divergent code bases performing similar or identical functions. Not only may customers experience inconsistent results, but it can also be very costly in terms of staffing, hardware and software.

But it doesn't have to be this way. A service-oriented architecture can address these shortcomings by enabling a capability known as process

SERVICES COMPOSITION CAN VARY BASED ON BUSINESS NEEDS AND TECHNOLOGICAL EXPERTISE, SUCH AS PROGRAMMING LANGUAGES AND SPECIALIZED MIDDLEWARE AND AVAILABLE RESOURCES. "

serving. This capability allows tasks, implemented as reusable services, to be composed into different patterns to create or modify business processes, thereby allowing a company to react quickly to changing business situations.

PROCESS SERVICES CONCEPTS

Services composition can vary based on business needs and technological expertise, such as programming languages, specialized middleware and available resources. The path a company follows will differ within and across industries, but it must account for a number of aspects based on the needs of the business and how it presents itself in the marketplace.

Some of these aspects include:
» The size of a company and the resources available to it
» The strengths and weaknesses of its IT staff
» Process availability
» Design flexibility

Regardless of which path a company follows, it will develop into an important enterprise function and must be managed as any other critical software asset. The quality of service (QoS) of the processes is a core consideration to address. Since many of these processes will reuse existing services and applications, there are real benefits to keeping the processes and the services they use integrated within the same environment. If most of the services are already on the mainframe, it makes good sense to host the processes there as well.

Processes can be created in several ways. Programs can be developed that embed the necessary navigation through a series of services, creating a composite application that defines a business process. These programs can be written in any language but are usually written in Java, COBOL or .net. Though they produce the desired result, the nature of the embedded logic will cause them to be both difficult to maintain and to have limited flexibility for augmentation.

These programs can also be written with specialized middleware that externalizes the flow through a business process. This will provide greater flexibility. Some of these specialized middleware products also provide the ability to define interactions through standards-based meta-data definitions. As mentioned previously, many of the tasks in these processes are done manually. As such, many of the meta-data-based middleware products define capabilities that include manual actions as part of process definitions.

Decisions on business process performance characteristics also need to be considered. They need to be based on business requirements and, perhaps, whether the process must be quickly completed or can be extended, the expected availability, expected usage volume and the required flexibility and adaptability to change. How a business answers these questions has a direct bearing on how their business process is composed and implemented. For example, a process that must be completed quickly and defines a standard set of unchange-

Regardless of which path a company follows, it will develop into an important **SOA SECRET** enterprise function and must be managed as any other critical software asset. The quality of service (QoS) of the processes is a core consideration to address.

EVEN IF AN ORGANIZATION HAS BEGUN TO AUTOMATE TASKS AS BUSINESS SERVICES WITHIN ITS SOA STRATEGY, IT IS NOT TAKING FULL ADVANTAGE OF THE SOA PARADIGM.

able tasks may be efficiently implemented by embedding it into application logic using a high-performance language in a server environment. However, this high level of performance, durability and longevity will be at the cost of reduced flexibility in change and adaptability.

Another option with a high degree of flexibility (but less efficiency) is specialized middleware, used to externalize the process flow. This will apply the process as a composition of multiple tasks (services) that can be altered, augmented or rearranged though meta-data. For example, if a process currently includes human actions that can be automated, the process can be quickly modified and redeployed without significant programming effort. If this meta-data approach is based on open standards like XML, meta definition standards and Java, efficiencies can be achieved by using technologies that manage the entire development cycle from process definition to runtime deployment. This is one of the key business value propositions of process serving.

The required skill sets for these two approaches differ substantially. The first approach, with its focus on performance, requires traditional development skills and all the appropriate tools used for code development, deployment, testing, debugging, etc. The second approach, with its focus on rapid deployment and flexibility, needs a different development methodology and skill set. GUI-styled construction tools are a core requirement. This non-code-based form of development moves application creation closer to the business and allows the developer to focus on meeting real business requirements rather than non-functional application coding. This is a major value proposition of the middleware approach.

A process-based approach also allows the developer to express the process several ways. One is as a flow chart, or Visio diagram. This development method visually depicts the major components of the process and graphically represents the relationship of one component to another. A process-based approach also allows the application to be expressed as event driven. In an event-driven process, tools can show each component in the process and the events that will trigger execution. The tools required for the construction of a business process model must allow them to be depicted and tailored to these various thought patterns. The ability to define a process in multiple ways is another important part of this business proposition.

FIRST STEPS

SOA does not imply business process serving, since business process serving does not require any form of automation or design around service-oriented architecture. Many business processes are still performed manually or are ingrained in inflexible, stovepipe applications. These processes are critical to running a particular line of business or to offering a new product or service.

Even if an organization has begun to automate tasks as business services within its SOA strategy, it is not taking full advantage of the SOA paradigm. The ultimate value of SOA is the ability to combine automated business services to create new market offerings that may

---

» SOA SECRET

An option with a high degree of flexibility (but less efficiency) is specialized middleware, used to externalize the process flow. This will apply the process as a composition of multiple tasks (services) that can be altered, augmented or rearranged though meta-data.

> ## NO MATTER HOW APPEALING THE BENEFITS, AN ENTERPRISE SHOULD NOT ATTACK A LARGE PROJECT QUICKLY. THIS IS TYPICALLY THE LEAST EFFECTIVE WAY TO ENTER SOA AND BUSINESS PROCESS SERVING.

reduce time-to-market and development costs. Through business process serving, a company can shift its focus to the enterprise-wide level and provide a consistent, flexible environment.

SOA is a business-centric IT architectural approach that integrates a company with linked, repeatable business tasks, or services. SOA is a foundation that allows businesses to build composite applications using services as building blocks. A business should take these steps to define and build their business processes by identifying:

» Existing core services that will be used as part of the processes
» Core processes for the business or line-of-business
» Services or processes that can be reused or shared by other processes, including higher order processes

The first step of building a business process is to determine the logical components of an application and/or current business process, then split them in a reusable fashion. This is not a trivial task, and appropriate time and resources need to be allocated. A failure to isolate reusable components could lead to reduced flexibility, increased cost and an environment more difficult to manage. When identifying components, it is important not to limit the focus to a particular business task or business area. It is likely that these functions and the data that these functions interact with are being performed by numerous areas across the organization. By factoring this information into the components' identification, a much higher degree of reuse can be achieved.

Paying attention to identifying these multiple sources for common information and determining how the eventual enterprise view of this data should appear will go far toward defining the components that will interact with this data.

Along with identifying core services is recognizing core business processes. A core business process has two parts: macro and micro. The macro process defines a complete end-to-end process that conducts a core business function or creates a product or service. This is the easier task. More difficult is identifying the micro processes. These will be an aggregation of reusable components. In essence, the smallest components that get defined as reusable services can be combined, first into reusable collections of components and then into a large-grain business process that can be defined and modified based on the needs of the enterprise.

No matter how appealing the benefits, an enterprise should not attack a large project quickly. This is typically the least effective way to enter SOA and business process serving. The tendency to start coding if a problem appears to be solvable through SOA usually leads to failed implementations. It is important to take a more cautious approach by starting small and learning from mistakes on low visibility projects. This will enable the creation of ground rules, roadmaps and blueprints that can provide the foundation for future, larger projects. The learning experience and documentation from these initial projects will aid a

In an event-driven process, tools can show each component in the process » **SOA SECRET** **and the events that will trigger execution. The tools required for the construction of a business process model must allow them to be depicted and tailored to these various thought patterns. The ability to define a process in multiple ways is another important part of this business proposition.**

company in defining a complete SOA and business process strategy that accounts for component definition, component combination, the infrastructure needed to support SOA and the necessary governance and policies.

A BIG COMPANY SOLUTION

Business process serving is not limited to large companies, but it can have it biggest benefits in that environment. This is not to say that a smaller company with a niche market focus cannot benefit from business process serving, especially if it can provide the ability to adapt and offer products and services to a global market. While the concepts in this book can equally apply to smaller companies, its primary focus is on larger companies that provide a range of internal and external products and services.

One advantage many large companies have is that they've already begun some form of componentization. These companies often have existing services that overlap because of a past acquisition or merger, or because they have a departmental/line-of business heritage that now needs an enterprise focus. They often have also started building an understanding of how their business can be broken into services and may have completed some work in logically separating business processes from data. They now need to take the next step: breaking the business logic apart into specific routines that can be used in different applications.

For example, a company's previous efforts may have identified five applications that implement "customer" in various forms. These five implementations individually create both an environment that is difficult to manage and potentially inconsistent views of what even constitutes a customer. However, the combination of these five implementations creates an excellent picture of what defines a customer to this enterprise. Evaluating the data and services that interact with this "customer" data will define a core set of services and business processes for the "customer," as well as how to interact with various portions of that customer data from an enterprise perspective. After an enterprise view of the customer is defined, the focus can then be on how to create a set of reusable service and process implementations that can be plugged into existing applications and utilized by new systems that also may need to interact with the customer data.

Much of this activity is more an intellectual than a programming exercise. However, the benefit of this activity rests in successfully implementing SOA and business process serving from an enterprise perspective. The ability to implement one "customer" that leverages the business knowledge contained in the original systems will help the enterprise realize the potential these technologies have to offer.

What may not be apparent is the increased importance the underlying infrastructure plays. Previously, each of these five implementations of "customer" was likely served from different infrastructure platforms with various degrees of scalability, flexibility and reliability. As a company moves from many implementations of logical services and processes to a single, enterprise-wide view, the capabilities of the infrastructure running these applications becomes more important. Additionally, the flexibility that this infrastructure offers should be able to provide different levels of service to users. Common infrastructure services like security, transactional integrity or state management and robust environmental management capabilities become increasingly

> **SOA SECRET**
>
> The first step of building a business process is to determine the logical components of an application and/or current business process, then split them in a reusable fashion. This is not a trivial task, and appropriate time and resources need to be allocated. A failure to isolate reusable components could lead to reduced flexibility, increased cost and an environment more difficult to manage.

SECURITY IS IMPORTANT FOR ANY APPLICATION. IT BECOMES MORE IMPORTANT AS SERVICES AND BUSINESS PROCESSES BECOME ACCESSIBLE FROM MANY DIFFERENT LOCATIONS.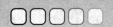

important. In the example, when "customer" was implemented as five unique instances, many of the "enhancements" from an environmental perspective appeared cost prohibitive because they would have to be implemented five times. However, as a direct benefit of consolidation, these increased advantages can also be provided at an enterprise level, gaining both advanced functionality and reduced cost.

QUALITY OF SERVICE

It is obvious that business applications will have a certain quality of service associated with them. These will vary based on technical and non-technical factors defined by the transactional characteristics of the workload, the ability to isolate problems if they arise, end-user performance response times and government regulations on data security and privacy. These and other characteristics will play a large part in the ability to successfully implement an SOA strategy and take advantage of business process serving.

Many of a company's existing assets already have a set of quality of service (QoS) characteristics specific to the needs of that particular application. However, as new and existing core business services are exposed—through an SOA-based methodology or toolset—and combined into new business processes to meet changing business requirements, a shared set of QoS characteristics will also need to be addressed to manage this flexible and changing environment. By not reviewing this new set of requirements and addressing them appropriately, a company places itself at risk by exposing its core business applications and potentially impacting ongoing operations.

QoS that should be reviewed before exposing business functionality of services include security, workload management, process state management and transactional capabilities. This list is just a starting point towards a more comprehensive review. Each business will be unique and have unique requirements. What is important is that a company carefully reviews these and other issues to ensure that needs are met.

Security
Security is important for any application. It becomes more important as services and business processes become accessible from many different locations. Requests for a process or service may be initiated by someone sitting in a front-end environment, such as a web browser, or it may be initiated through a system-to-system interaction via a web service call. This interaction may also enter via a synchronous protocol such as HTTP, or asynchronously via Java Messaging Service (JMS).

As a request flows through a process, it may also pass through several interactions. At each of these, the request crosses a security domain boundary and initiates an entire set of questions on the mechanisms to employ for authorization and authentication. As the process continues with requests for other services like SAP, IMS or CICS, more security boundaries are crossed. The issue then becomes how to federate the different security and policy management strategies. Since the security products and management policies for each request may differ, a strategy is needed to ensure that credentials can be either mapped or allowed to flow as they pass from one security boundary to the next. Making these disparate security products provide a single, consistent view is important so that what occurs from an end-to-end perspective is consistent and intended. Some of these concerns are mitigated, although not eliminated, when the deployment of the

process logic is within the same physical environment. For example, composite applications deployed in a mainframe environment can all be managed under the same security product. The interactions between the services that make up the business process will be consistent throughout the flow regardless of whether these interactions are synchronous, asynchronous or over a variety of protocols.

Workload Management

As previously discussed, the nature of creating business services and composing them into business processes will result in multiple access paths based on a variety of factors. For instance, a company makes a service available through its externally facing Internet site. This service is accessed directly by the public and business partners. From the company's viewpoint, when the service is initiated by a business partner, it is to be given the highest level of service. When accessed by anyone else, adequate resources are devoted, but not at the expense of any business partner-related work. This is difficult to resolve and might even involve deploying the service across multiple hardware platforms that provide a different QoS.

It gets even more complicated when subsequent classifications are applied to the initiation of the service. For example, when the exposed service is implemented as a composite business process using multiple back-end services, there should be a consistent means to assign resources to associated tasks. Additionally, this ability should be distinct from other paths that may use some of the same reusable components and be dynamically manageable. A process that is distributed across multiple hardware and software platforms is unlikely to have the original classification automatically flow from one component to the next. There is also the potential for the workload management mechanisms to interfere with each other, with unpredictable results. Again, the ability to provide an end-to-end solution to categorize and classify varying workloads is either not possible or extremely difficult to manage in a distributed environment.

To address these needs, process logic and services can be consolidated into one physical environment that provides the ability to host J2EE, CICS or IMS services and data access services along with the ability to construct and serve business processes. This consolidation can enable a company to achieve a consistent and efficient means of maximizing resource utilization and maintain service-level commitments. It also allows categorization and classification to be done in a centralized, dynamic manner.

Process State Management

A process can have many characteristics. It can be long-running or it can be short and atomic. As a business service navigates the steps in the process, it maintains the state of the process, such as: current activity of the process; process local data/variables; transactional state; and activity history in some sort of repository, usually a database. For large enterprise customers, that database, whether it's DB2, Oracle or some other, is traditionally located on a mainframe system that's good at transferring and serving large volumes of data. Storing the process state in a database that is not in the same environment, especially when that state is using services in the back-end mainframe environment, is not an acceptable alternative for most users. The potential overhead involved in constantly transferring the state data over the net-

» SOA SECRET

As new and existing core business services are exposed—through an SOA-based methodology or toolset—and combined into new business processes to meet changing business requirements, a shared set of QoS characteristics will also need to be addressed to manage this flexible and changing environment. By not reviewing this new set of requirements and addressing them appropriately, a company places itself at risk by exposing its core business applications and potentially impacting ongoing operations.

> **WHEN TALKING ABOUT PROCESS SERVING, IT IS NECESSARILY IMPORTANT TO DISCUSS THE MANAGEMENT OF AN SOA STRATEGY AND ENVIRONMENT.**

work to a remote system could have performance implications, particularly as the volume of process initiations increases.

Where the database resides also impacts outage recovery. An outage within the system interacting with the business process should not affect that process's ability to continue. If a failure occurs during the execution of a business process and the database is served remotely, there may be a need to synchronize the state data within the database with the current state of the business process. This is done to recover or restart the execution of the business process and ensure that the work and data was not left in an indeterminate state. In the case of a local database, this situation can be handled automatically through local restart and recovery, or through the ability to share data across multiple mainframe systems.

Transactional Capabilities
The standards that support processes also support two types of transactional capabilities: two-phase commit atomic; and compensating. These capabilities are focused on what to do when a failure occurs. When the process is first invoked, there will be some transactional context surrounding it. This context will support the creation of a new atomic transaction, inherit transactional behavior from its initiator or some form of compensation logic. As the process executes, it will try to propagate its transactional state to the services it is using in back-end systems. Some of these back-end systems will support a two-phase commit transactional protocol from the process server to the back end.

If all the services support two-phase commit transactions, a mid-stream failure can be handled in a well orchestrated manner. If the impacted services do not support that processing and they involve multiple back-end updates, a compensating transaction must be employed. This is one method of handling failures, but it's sometimes necessary and must only be implemented as a last resort. It is important to note that while the before and after state data in a two-phase commit transaction is stored locally on the database server, in a compensating transaction this data must be managed locally to the application or business process. Therefore, if a failure occurs that requires a compensating transaction, this recovery would need a network transfer of data to restore the original state.

INFRASTRUCTURE CAPABILITIES

Infrastructure capabilities that play an important role with SOA services include: system automation; operations and console support; high availability and disaster recovery; logging and auditing; scale and cluster support.

System Automation

Many large customers have a system automation product to manage and respond to events within the environment where services reside. When SOA creates processes, they become new applications which will be targets for system automation management. Process components from different technology platforms already have their own existing system automation product(s) and policies. The company managing this will then have to determine how to define policies in both environments that correlate with the overall behavior required from this service.

Operations and Console Support

Should the existing services and the new processes be deployed onto different environments, the operations and consoles will be totally different even if they feed into the same physical console because of the different skill sets required to manage multiple environments.

AN OUTAGE WITHIN THE SYSTEM INTERACTING WITH THE BUSINESS PROCESS SHOULD NOT AFFECT THAT PROCESS'S ABILITY TO CONTINUE.

High Availability and Disaster Recovery

If composed SOA services/processes and their existing core services are deployed on different environments, there emerges the issues of how to synchronize updates and monitor the checkpoints being used for disaster recovery and high availability, and to coordinate the different recovery polices. The service could now have multiple detection mechanisms to determine outages operating across the component's platforms. If the service stays within a similar technology platform, it will have a detection mechanism that can identify the scope of an outage and a common recovery policy.

Logging and Auditing/Scale and Cluster Support

Companies have separate requirements for auditing or logging the behavior of transactions defined within business processes. As boundaries are crossed, different audit logs will have to be correlated. When processes are on different platforms, then the correlation of the logs becomes more difficult.

An organization's cluster support is defined for existing services. An important aspect of those existing services is that they've been exposed to SOA through these business processes. This doesn't mean that the workload that they are handling is a new demand driven by these business processes; rather, it's an additional aspect to the workload they were already handling. However, many systems have a scaling mechanism on back-end resources which reacts to workload availability. If that differs from what exists on the front-end resource, then there is an issue with how to manage and coordinate the addition or subtraction of resources in an end-to-end cluster environment.

MANAGEMENT

When talking about process serving, it is necessarily important to discuss the management of an SOA strategy and environment. These topics relate to how all aspects of an SOA are managed, from setting business requirements through the entire lifecycle of definition, creation, deployment, runtime environment, maintenance and sunset.

Policy and Procedures

Without policies and procedures to document a service's definitions and registrations, its lifecycle and how different stages interact, a company can quickly find that overlapping services are being created. Soon, a company may find it is quickly returning to the application environment that SOA was to replace. This is primarily a non-technical exercise, but there are tools that will aid a company in managing available services. One of these tools is a service registry. This could easily be included as an infrastructure capability, but it plays an important role in the management of services. These tools should be able to provide the ability to locate services, store service meta-data and provide mechanisms to aid in management and promote reuse. Tools like this can be a great aid in managing a growing service-based environ-

> » **SOA SECRET**
>
> The ability to manage change at several layers can be enhanced when they all reside on a common platform like the mainframe. In part, the capabilities of this environment have been built over decades of serving large enterprise business applications. The ability to change the hardware and operating system rapidly in a clustered environment without effecting the continuous operation of the business has existed for a long time.

ment, but they should not be relied upon to replace a well defined governance policy.

Standards

Many standards relate to SOA, like those for web services and process serving. It is clear that as a company forms an SOA strategy and begins implementing business process serving, it must base its own foundation around industry standards. The platform chosen to provide that foundation should adhere to recognized standards. From an enterprise perspective, it is important for a company to define which standards it will follow and understand the ramifications of those choices. Companies should also define standards that must be adhered to within their own environments, including limitations and outright bans. Without standards, a company can implement an SOA strategy that does not allow for growth, limits flexibility and increases the cost of ownership.

Maintenance and Versioning

Applications, services and business processes are not static. Middleware, operating systems and hardware are not static. Even industry standards and best practices change over time. However, companies cannot be shackled by change. They cannot risk exposing core business processes to changes that could result in lost customers or business opportunities. Balancing change with potential business risks is a basic challenge as companies move to an SOA and process-serving environment. Unlike the intellectual exercises of defining policies, procedures and standards, the ability to manage change effectively requires strong technical understanding of how business components interact, how change can be introduced and how the capabilities of the underlying middleware, operating system and hardware can be used in support.

From a business process or services viewpoint, change in the SOA paradigm has the potential to impact any composite application that utilizes them. In a stovepipe approach, it was common to take the entire application offline, remove the old version, install the new version and bring the application back online. This was acceptable when applications had limited interaction with other applications. However, it is not okay to take down all of a company's applications that utilize a service simply because that service is being changed. Likewise, it is not feasible to require all applications that interact with this service to change because that service is now incompatible. While it is technically easy to build multiple, parallel environments to allow the deployment of multiple service versions, the cost of this solution quickly outweighs any benefits accrued from SOA or business process serving.

Change also impacts every other layer, including application-serving middleware, database, operating system and underlying hardware. Change in these layers cannot be disruptive and cannot effect the continuous operation of the business. These lower layers must support redundancy and be able to stage migrations to new versions without a loss of service to the customer. It is important for a company to evaluate the capabilities of each layer and build a solution that provides a robust, continuously available environment that supports change.

The ability to manage change at several layers can be enhanced when they all reside on a common platform like the mainframe. In part, the capabilities of this environment have been built over decades of serving large enterprise business applications. The ability to change the hardware and operating system rapidly in a clustered environment without effecting the continuous operation of the business has existed for a long time. The middleware that most companies use in this environment also supports a staged migration of change, both at a middleware and business application layer. In many cases, these changes can be introduced concurrently without risk of interference. These features that have been relied upon are the same features that extend to an SOA and business process serving environment. An additional ben-

efit is that by limiting the number of variants from an infrastructural perspective, a company can reduce the amount of specialized staffing experts necessary to support it.

Terry Borden is a senior technical staff member in the IBM Software Group Strategy and Technology area at IBM Somers. He joined IBM in 1970 and during his career has worked in mainframe (System 360 onward) architecture and development and in IBM's Software Group in the area of messaging and business integration. His work has included operating systems, transaction processing, high availability, clustering, messaging and business integration.

Bill Mitlehner is a senior technology architect at Aetna and manages its Web Technologies organization. For the past 6 years, he has been focused on web technologies on the z/OS and distributed platforms, developing strategies for implementing distributed applications and services across large enterprise environments. He has worked in the IT industry since the early 80s on distributed and mainframe environments designing and implementing solutions involving a wide variety of operating system and middleware solutions.

Chapter

5

THE PHYSICALLY INTEGRATED ENTERPRISE

For the many organizations investing in or contemplating a distributed server environment, it may be time to reconsider the mainframe environment, particularly when it comes to implementing a service-oriented architecture.
This chapter discusses the advantages.

BY MARTIN KENNEDY

The two prominent service delivery models are the mainframe environment and the distributed server environment. The highly virtualized mainframe leverages components; the distributed server environment, for the most part, does not. Instead, it consists of individual servers, each usually applied to one specific function such as web connectivity, applications, database, etc. This chapter is a discussion of the differences in these two delivery models.

Over the last few years there's been a tendency to migrate many applications over to distributed servers, believing these systems were easy to deploy and support with ample software and skilled IT staff. Now, this tendency to use more and more servers is beginning to stress a company's ability to cost effectively house and run them. Implementing service-oriented architecture infrastructures, specifically with the adoption of Enterprise Service Bus (ESB) runtimes and the capacity that these runtimes require, will only serve to provide additional stress to these environments.

INFRASTRUCTURE NEEDS

Compared to the distributed servers set up within an enterprise, a mainframe environment has substantial infrastructure advantages that begin literally with the floor space and power needed to deploy the technology and include other factors such as manpower requirements and security.

Space and Power

The floor space required to house distributed systems is beginning to cause organizations considerable pain. Each server deployed in a data center has a footprint. There is also a fair amount of ancillary infrastructure needed to connect these distributed servers to storage subsystems and networks, which translates into more switches, routers and hubs. All of this equipment takes up a large amount of floor space. Powering all of these devices requires power distribution units and generators since each commercial data processing environment must have uninterrupted power sources. This entire complex infrastructure comes with significant expense.

The cost of power in distributed server environments is becoming an even more critical issue. In New York City, for example, the expectation is that electricity costs will rise from 11 cents a kilowatt-hour in 2006 to 17 cents per kilowatt hour in 2007, a 55% increase — and a trend that is likely to continue. Companies in major metropolitan areas in North America are fortunate in that the power utilities can usually keep up with the power demand, and they can build out datacenters and continue to power them, albeit at higher costs. This is not necessarily the case everywhere. Many companies outside major metropolitan areas have met with their power utility companies to discuss their requirements and have raised concerns that utility companies are not in a position to provide large increases in capacity without investing heavily in their own infrastructure. This substantially limits a company's ability to expand server farms to meet business requirements and timelines.

In contrast, a mainframe is a virtual environment, its space needs are less and its power needs are lower and grow at a much smaller pace. Within one mainframe image, thousands of web services can be run, all on just a few floor tiles in the datacenter. As for power consumption, a mainframe consumes about 25 watts per square foot compared to some 75 watts per square foot for the typical server. Blade centers are even larger power consumers at 125 watts per square foot. All of this power usage ultimately translates into heat that has to be removed by a chiller plant that also requires significant power and infrastructure, thus compounding the problem.

Staffing

Over and above space and power are staffing needs. In a distributed environment there are teams dedicated to individual applications and workloads. With distributed servers often running only one application, staffing requirements can be substantial. In a mainframe environment, a high level of standardization can allow support teams to be leveraged against all the application workloads that a particular technical discipline supports. WebSphere and database support in the mainframe environment are good examples of this.

In part, the proliferation of distributed servers was prompted by the perception that they are easy to deploy, and quite cost-effective, utilizing plenty of off-the-shelf software products and programmers straight out of college. But as server farms grew, so did the complexity to support them. In the typical support organization, there are many people involved in the actual racking, stacking and provisioning of a server. There are people who specialize in putting floor infrastructure and cabinets together; people who specialize in power; and people who specialize in zoning storage area networks (SANs), getting the cabling done, provisioning network ports, defining subnets and getting IP addresses assigned and managed. After the physical installation is complete, the operating system needs to be installed, and specialized security software has to be layered on top of

> **IN MANY COMPANIES, A SERVER ORDERED TODAY WILL NOT BE ONLINE, TO THE POINT WHERE THE APPLICATIONS CAN BE INSTALLED, FOR MONTHS.**

Windows and UNIX to make it secure. That also takes time, people and money. In many companies, a server ordered today will not be online, to the point where the applications can be installed, for months. In addition, in some facilities, old systems need to be de-installed to make room for new ones.

These issues don't exist in the mainframe environment. Virtual servers can be provisioned in hours on a mainframe, and capacity can be added dynamically without taking applications down.

It's not until a thousand servers are installed that organizations really focus on server costs — how to fit them in the building, meet growing power requirements, mitigate security risks, etc. Then there's maintaining adequate staffing to care and feed the enormous infrastructure required, not to mention continually addressing security, compliance issues, disaster recovery and backup.

Security
There is a profound difference between the security architecture implemented in the mainframe versus distributed servers. The server virtualization technologies behind System z mainframes have received high security ratings based on the Common Criteria specifications that are becoming a standard in the IT industry. The Evaluation Assurance Level rating of 5 (EAL5) on the logical partitions of the System z9 EC (Enterprise Class) mainframe is remarkable; in fact, so far only IBM's mainframe partitions have attained this rating.

Beyond the hardware itself the security infrastructure in a mainframe running z/OS has a National Computer Security Center (NCSC) rating of B1. Distributed UNIX servers, on the other hand, receive a security infrastructure rating of C2 (C1 at best). These national security ratings are similar to the Richter scale where the difference between a C and a B is large. Most distributed UNIX environments require a significant amount of add-on technology to provide an adequately secure environment. In many cases, these add-ons must be procured from multiple vendors, thereby increasing maintenance and support complexity.

Another fundamental difference between mainframe z/OS security and distributed UNIX security is that it's difficult to limit what a system administrator has access to in the distributed world. The UNIX security model relies heavily on data grouping and "access control lists." System administrators are frequently required to log on with a UNIX User Identity (UID) of zero and become a "super user." These users have access to everything, not just the resources they need to work on. This has always been troubling because a simple mistake could have catastrophic results.

A mainframe is a virtual environment, its space needs are less and its power **» SOA SECRET** needs are lower and grow at a much smaller pace. Within one mainframe image, thousands of web services can be run, all on just a few floor tiles in the datacenter. As for power consumption, a mainframe consumes about 25 watts per square foot compared to a server's some 75 watts per square foot. Blade centers are even larger power consumers at 125 watts per square foot. All of this power usage ultimately translates into heat that has to be removed by a chiller plant that also requires significant power and infrastructure, thus compounding the problem.

In a mainframe environment, there is an enormous level of access granularity. Even with UNIX services on the mainframe systems, programmers do not need to use a UID of zero after the system is built; they just don't need access to everything. The mainframe security model allows programmers to be locked down into specialized IDs where access is limited and everything they do can be audited. And unlike distributed UNIX systems, the mainframe is auditable at a highly granular level. In a distributed UNIX system, audit trails are relatively limited even when all the add-on tools are applied; it's just at the level of watching users typing on a screen or "keystroke logging." This is viewing an action, not the event that the action caused. On a mainframe running z/OS, auditing at the actual event level, not the command level, is possible. If a file is altered, a record reflecting that alteration of that file is produced. If a permission bit or ownership is changed on a file, a record of that modification is produced.

INSTALLED VS. USED CAPACITY

In general, many planning assumptions of five or six years ago were simply wrong. Organizations are now beginning to confront infrastructure issues as they try to get a datacenter built but cannot get all the power they need to run it. How much equipment is bought versus actually used is becoming an important issue. Most distributed servers from a CPU perspective are underutilized, sometimes significantly underutilized. A mainframe environment by comparison typically uses all of its installed capacity.

The nature of the distributed environment lends it to underutilization. Studies have shown that CPU utilization is commonly below 30%, and twice the data storage is often needed to deliver the same functionality in a distributed server environment as in a mainframe one. This condition is essentially because distributed servers were designed as single application systems. Hence, the notion of serialization, or the ability to share physical data, doesn't exist across the distributed space. Distributed servers were not designed to share physical resources with each other. As a result, every server must have enough disk storage to satisfy its worst-case scenario. The result is a vast amount of allocated storage that most of the time is doing nothing. If that storage could all be shared, one server's peaks would fill another server's valleys. This type of sharing is not only possible but easy to implement on a mainframe; not so on a distributed server.

Since nothing is physically shared across distributed server boundaries, every time more storage capacity is needed, it must be added. This involves procuring the storage space, then "zoning" and allocating it to the server. The utilization problem is further complicated because that storage can only be added in large-grained minimum increments.

For example, a disk subsystem consists of logical units of disk storage (LUNs). LUN sizes need to be predetermined and are hard-configured into the storage subsystem when it's installed. Most storage administrators limit the number of LUN sizes in order to facilitate the management of the storage farm. As an example, an environment may support three sizes of LUNs: small ones of 36 gigabytes; mid-size of 72 gigabytes; and large at 147 gigabytes. When a user's web server needs only 3 gigabytes, he or she must buy at least 36 gigabytes. Hence 33 gigabytes of storage will be doing nothing. When

Studies have shown that CPU utilization is commonly below 30%, and » **SOA SECRET** **twice the data storage is often needed to deliver the same functionality in a distributed server environment as in a mainframe one. This condition is essentially because distributed servers were designed as single application systems. Hence, the notion of serialization, or the ability to share physical data, doesn't exist across the distributed space. Servers were not designed to share physical resources with another server.**

you examine this condition across thousands of servers and file systems you can easily find vast amounts of unutilized storage. The problem gets worse in a disaster recovery scenario. Inefficiencies at the primary site get mirrored to a disaster recovery site, where there is often an extra copy for testing.

An enormous amount of server capacity can be put into a single mainframe and run in the same operating system stack. This approach allows the servers to leverage the entire I/O infrastructure. A distributed server, in contrast, has dedicated infrastructure for I/O that cannot effectively be leveraged. In sum, the whole notion of allocated versus actually used storage factors heavily into the true cost of a "usable byte" of data.

There are things that can be and are being done in a distributed system to improve utilization, but they are not easy to do. There is some opportunity to improve server performance with virtualization technologies, but it will be extremely difficult to achieve the level of virtualization possible on a mainframe. z/OS images can and do run regularly at 100%.

The infrastructure cost of servers, power, cooling and floor space, over time, could easily exceed the cost of the distributed servers themselves. Meeting this challenge will cause an organization to embrace the virtualization technologies of the mainframe, as well as explore cost-effective and practical ways to increase distributed server utilization and — most importantly — learn how to select the right platform for its requirements.

The mainframe is a real option that's here today. When you consider that a large percentage of an organization's core data still resides on this platform, it's only logical that the mainframe has the greatest capability for re-use, compared to other platforms. When creating SOA services — be they J2EE services, CICS services, etc. — if the data resides on the mainframe, it's logical to have the service exposed on the mainframe to minimize application and data path lengths and to maximize reliability and performance.

The mainframe's cost-effectiveness continues to improve. In addition, IBM has introduced specialized processors, called zAAPs (System z Application Assist Processors), which are designed to run Java. The zAAP is an economical piece of hardware with no associated software costs. Since software represents the biggest piece of the pie in terms of mainframe costs, running Java-based applications on the mainframe using zAAPs is an attractive choice. A similar product, zIIPs (System z Integrated Information Processors), are designed to offload specialized processing. DB2 is the first exploiter of this technology that will greatly reduce the cost of running certain types of database applications.

UPGRADING

Through every computer system's life cycle there is always a hardware upgrade. Most computers and computer peripherals operate on a three- to four-year cycle at which time there is a natural upgrade to newer hardware. For the past 30 years, companies have been able to change out a mainframe for a newer model without changing one line of application code. For the most part, applications written in 1975 are running today on the latest mainframe. That's not the case with distributed systems, where upgrading is typically a difficult undertaking.

System administrators are frequently required to log on with a UNIX User Identity (UID) of zero and become a "super user." **» SOA SECRET** These users have access to everything, not just the resource they need to work on. This has always been troubling because a simple mistake could have catastrophic results.

In a distributed system, it's extremely difficult and somewhat risky to upgrade the operating system on a distributed server. The application, the component products and the operating system are often tightly coupled. In many cases, the operating system cannot be upgraded without a real risk of breaking the application. To compound the problem, operating system upgrades are often a prerequisite to installing the latest generation hardware. Large distributed environments often have hundreds of servers that can't be upgraded without a major effort by both the system administrators and the applications staff. The approach to the problem usually involves buying new hardware, installing the new operating systems and then rebuilding and testing the application from scratch.

With a mainframe, the datacenter staff can usually do the entire upgrade without impacting applications.

SOFTWARE INTEGRATION

When implementing infrastructures to support SOA, components from different vendors must be glued together or "integrated." Whenever one of those components changes, the entire service must be tested to verify that the changed component still integrates with all the other components. This integration testing usually requires the participation of multiple vendors. This process can take a long time and requires significant coordination on the part of all vendors. A large quantity of human resources and time is absorbed in keeping current with technology.

The mainframe environment, because of its far fewer physical components, presents far less of an integration problem. In addition, the mainframe already has a nice supply of fully integrated re-useable services There's a mountain of services buried in mainframe: the applications that run many core businesses today, including thousands of CICS transactions; services running in Java containers; WebSphere MQ and WebSphere Message Broker services, etc. These services could easily be integrated and exposed to become consumers or providers in an SOA web services implementation, and plug directly into an ESB.

BUDGETING

The traditional mainframe datacenter historically has had a centralized budget. Users were charged for the machine cycles and the storage that they used. This centralized model resulted in datacenters with large budgets. When distributed servers were introduced, many organizations started putting them in without a mature, formal process for measuring and charging for support. For all intents and purposes, many users just paid for the capital expense and received a free ride on datacenter space, people support, software support and other services that often got buried in the organization's mainframe budget. Hence, it was not uncommon for the mainframe budgets to have covered many distributed server expenses. This practice led many users to perceive that mainframes were expensive, and it fueled the notion that distributed servers were a less expensive alternative.

Over time, however, organizations have begun to focus carefully on the actual cost of ownership. And when that focus takes into account floor space, power, cooling, people, server utilization, change management, disaster recovery, security, vulnerability and patch management, storage management and backup, not to mention the real cost of software and system upgrades, the picture begins to change. Once all the

When implementing infrastructures to support SOA, components from different vendors must be glued together or "integrated." Whenever one of those components changes, the entire service must be tested to verify that the changed component still integrates with all the other components. That integration testing usually requires the participation of multiple vendors.

» **SOA SECRET**

costs are appropriately assigned, distributed servers no longer look like a clear bargain. The more analysis conducted on the datacenter cost, the more standard beliefs are debunked.

OVERCOMING INERTIA

Unfortunately, once a large degree of momentum within an industry moves toward a specific technology, myth, legends and basic misconceptions emerge that influence future actions. Numerous vendor relationships arise and many application developers become focused on a particular technology or a particular way of doing things. Their perspective and scope is limited in many cases to delivering a specific functionality. An organization then may find it difficult to collectively step back and look at the big picture. Even when it does, it's often difficult to rapidly effect the changes needed to address the problem.

It's also difficult to convince people to change their behavior, especially when they're part of large organizations heavily entrenched in a particular way of doing things. SOA is forcing organizations to rethink the way they conduct business and how they build applications in support of business processes. Similarly, SOA is forcing IT deployment people to think strategically as well. Many will find that a more integrated, centralized approach is far better for an SOA solution.

When a company starts to scale to a large level, the aches and pains described in this chapter start to surface — problems not obvious at the beginning surface and dominate the time of the datacenter's management teams. Prior to Y2K, many companies did not even know how many servers they really had. It wasn't until it was thought that the servers might not work over the turn of the century that companies asked for an inventory. In the past six years, organizations have come to better identify the true costs and appropriate security infrastructure and tools to manage the environment.

LEGACY? WHAT LEGACY?

Financial entrepreneur Steve Forbes, at a recent commencement address, attributed the success of companies like Wal-Mart to the use of the mainframe computer. Forbes pointed out that the genius of Sam Walton was that he understood the power of information, and he knew how to deploy a piece of technology that was invented to help the military after the second world war against his needs to manage information. This leveraging of the mainframe helped propel Wal-Mart well ahead of its competitors. The same is true today. To be successful with SOA, organizations must learn how to pick the right platforms for their needs. Beyond the hype, many of the things we take for granted wouldn't function without mainframes. While many web sites run on distributed servers, it's not uncommon to find the core data they depend on still sits on a mainframe somewhere. Even with all the attempts to migrate applications off of mainframes, airline ticket purchases, ATM machines, credit cards services and many of our favorite web sites would not function without mainframes.

The key to success with SOA implementations is to know when, where and how to use both distributed servers and mainframes to achieve the most cost-effective, reliable and scalable result. In general, distributed servers need to be far more efficient, and organizations also need to start embracing technologies like the mainframe and

The infrastructure cost of servers, power, cooling and floor space, over » **SOA SECRET** **time, could easily exceed the cost of the distributed servers themselves. Meeting this challenge will cause organization to embrace the virtualization technologies of the mainframe, as well as explore cost effective and practical ways to increase distributed server utilization and most importantly learn how to select the right platform for their requirements.**

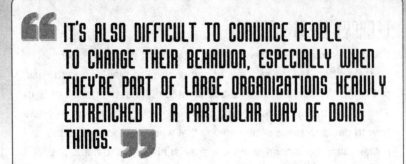

IT'S ALSO DIFFICULT TO CONVINCE PEOPLE TO CHANGE THEIR BEHAVIOR, ESPECIALLY WHEN THEY'RE PART OF LARGE ORGANIZATIONS HEAVILY ENTRENCHED IN A PARTICULAR WAY OF DOING THINGS.

leverage the wealth of rich, reliable application code that's already there. Putting the right applications back on the mainframe will allow companies to implement highly secure environments that can readily scale and take full advantage of inexpensive processors without the substantial infrastructure and cost overhead associated with it.

Martin Kennedy has worked in the banking and financial services industry for more than 30 years. He has worked extensively in the areas of application development and large scale enterprise system engineering and management. He is currently Director of Technical Service for Citigroup.

Chapter

◻ ◻ ⑥ ◻ ◻

THE INTELLIGENT SOA MANAGEMENT HUB

SOA, at its foundation, is managed not unlike any other large, complex workload. But there are differences in systems management necessary to make this new technology work at its best.

BY GEORGE GALAMBOS

E ver since systems management has been established as an independent discipline, for every new technology wave and the attendant design concepts the questions are posed: Is its management different from any previous technologies? Are there new aspects, new processes and objects to be monitored and managed? If the answer is affirmative, are there requirements, which would suggest a new way of implementing the management processes?

Systems based upon SOA as a combination of new design concepts and technologies are no different and, thus, these questions must be posed.

It suffices to state that the systems management for SOA will still focus on the traditional disciplines of change and problem management, monitoring and collecting information on problems and failures, managing performance and capacity, etc. Yet, the broad reach of SOA-based systems and the new business domains where SOA will be deployed also means more

SOA MANAGEMENT, AT ITS FOUNDATION, IS NOT SIGNIFICANTLY DIFFERENT FROM SYSTEM MANAGEMENT OF ANY OTHER LARGE WORKLOAD.

emphasis on security. Additionally, the higher profile role will raise the complexity of performance, problem and change management, as well as significantly extend the joint management of business and IT outcomes. Concomitant with these changes, there is more emphasis on the security and reliability of the platforms and technologies underlying SOA's systems management as a result, such as SOA's enhanced role in the enterprise's compliance with regulatory requirements.

Thus, this chapter will briefly explore the new systems management functions, the expectations raised by these functions to the underlying platform and then match those expectations with a well established yet promising technology. These expectations are: high availability for the systems management server; the ability to deal with very high volumes of systems management events; and an environment of enhanced security.

SOA management, at its foundation, is not significantly different from system management of any other large workload. But there are unique requirements that surface with SOA, which were either absent or unidentified for other workloads, such as on-line transaction processing (OLTP), client-server computing and others. This uniqueness can be summarized as follows:

1. SOA systems are frequently created as heterogeneous, broadly distributed systems.
2. Consequently, SOA introduces a much higher degree of variability in how hard these systems are driven. It is very difficult to establish a

"stable" or "static" consumption pattern. This makes it even more important to have a management system that is able to detect overloads quickly and respond appropriately. Without such a system business services will fail to meet expectations.

3. Finally, traditional component and systems monitoring and management is extended by monitoring and management of the business process and its outcome, supported by the SOA system. Business takes a direct interest in the behavior of IT systems, thus significantly increasing the stakes and the expectations of the management system.

SERVICE LEVEL MANAGEMENT: AVAILABILITY

For the sake of simplicity, it is postulated here that other systems management disciplines — e.g., change and problem management — all serve the purpose of providing reliable service that is ultimately implementing the discipline of availability management. Traditionally and particularly in non-SOA[1] systems, many enterprises, when observing and managing system service levels, were looking at the problem of components' availability as opposed to provided services. While the component view on availability (and system management at large) is being slowly phased out in the pre-SOA systems, it has been justified by the fact that in these systems the number of components frequently

> **» SOA SECRET**
>
> While the component view on availability (and system management at large) is being slowly phased out in the pre-SOA systems, it has been justified by the fact that in these systems the number of components frequently make up a single stack of hardware, software and application code. Focusing on a pervasive component and serving multiple applications — e.g., server, operating system or OLTP software — generally yielded a good base for stability, when combined with the focus of individual, application-specific components.

make up a single stack of hardware, software and application code. Focusing on a pervasive component and serving multiple applications — e.g., server, operating system or OLTP software — generally yielded a good base for stability, when combined with the focus of individual, application-specific components.

The component-based view on service level management will not serve SOA systems well. In the SOA world, multiple applications running on multiple disparate platforms often cooperate to create one outcome.[2]

The most interesting services are formed by the combination (composition) of simpler SOA services, to provide a higher value capability. These are often referred to as business services. The availability (and other characteristics) of these business services then is influenced by all its constituent services, themselves dependent on a large number of application and technology components. This requires a holistic approach, which is concerned with the entire application and system stack, multiple instances of which make up the business service. That means that the hardware, the impacted segments of the network, the operating system and the middleware are all serving as the foundations for the business service's operation. This "extended" stack frequently encompasses multiple devices, creating the potential for a heterogeneous collection of computing environments and services that may or may not run in the same datacenter, the same division or even in the same corporation, but all serving the particular outcome of that business service.

Thus, what is required is a management capability that reaches across organizational or technological entities that may be under different operational management. These circumstances lead to a management process and design, which is much more complex than non-SOA system management, even though the fundamental disciplines are the same. Performance management, change management, problem man-

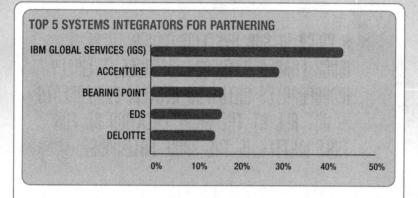

TOP 5 SYSTEMS INTEGRATORS FOR PARTNERING

agement, software configuration management and asset management are all exercised for the individual stacks, but the operational bar has been raised significantly for the whole.

This extended scope of management capability needs to be matched with the right computing resources serving that task. Whenever management action is taken in steady state, whether it is backup/restore, a change distribution or coherent security asserted over multiple services, it would require significant amounts of computing resources operating over equally large amounts of systems management data. The vastly increased scale of data (and information derived from it) potentially acquired from distinct organizations is another unique aspect of systems management in the SOA world. The management

» **SOA SECRET**

Whenever management action is taken in steady state, whether it is backup/ restore, a change distribution or coherent security asserted over multiple services, it would require significant amounts of computing resources operating over equally large amounts of systems management data. The vastly increased scale of data (and information derived from it) potentially acquired from distinct organizations is another unique aspect of systems management in the SOA world.

> ❝ A CMDB IN SOA SYSTEMS TENDS TO BE A MUCH LARGER DATABASE, BECAUSE IT LIKELY INCORPORATES DATA FOR SYSTEM COMPONENTS — NOT ALL AT THE SAME LOCATION OR FOR THAT MATTER IN THE SAME ENTERPRISE. ❞

of the collection and storage of this data is well suited to the Configuration Management Data Base (CMDB). A CMDB in SOA systems tends to be a much larger database, because it likely incorporates data for system components — not all at the same location or for that matter in the same enterprise.

These considerations gain importance in the midst of failure and recovery. Outages can be caused in an SOA-based application by failures in multiple computing activities that might have operated either in parallel or in sequence. Successful remediation of the SOA systems' outage requires the continuous collection of monitoring and event data and the correlation of those in order to narrow the possible causes of failure quickly. This requires a number of parallel activities and operational tasks, working with various data sources, to be pulled together. Data kept within a central repository, combined with the correlation analysis' result, will then be better able to identify the point of failure. All of this combination would have to be accomplished in a short period, thus a vast amount of computing power would be drawn upon. Then, the recovery action, be it automatic or governed by an operator, will call upon potentially significant processing power to control the orderly restoration of data and systems components. It is hence easy to see why the amount of data and the requisite computing capacity to process it in the systems management context would grow significantly for the SOA systems.

In summary, management of availability for SOA-based systems would need to support more complex processes than required in a traditional distributed system. Underlying these management processes, an execution environment is required that provides a very stable platform and a large amount of processing power to manage a large amount of data. It is also important that much of the management information has been collected and is being governed by this central facility.

SERVICE LEVEL MANAGEMENT: PERFORMANCE

Many of the considerations presented for availability management apply for performance as well. As an aside, it is important to note that outages frequently are caused by events, which themselves fall in the domain of performance management.

The performance (response time) of the business service (made up of one or more SOA services) is dependent on the proper design and capacity planning of a large number of components, many of them conceivably under another division's or corporate management. Service level agreements may well exist between the consumer (composer) of these services and the providers, be they in different divisions or organizations. Still, there is a need for proactive tracking and, if necessary, intervention or request for intervention in order to maintain the expected service level. This meticulous attention and readiness to act require broad-based monitoring and instantaneous correlation of collected data, creating yet another requirement for substantial computing and data management capacity.

BUSINESS PROCESS MANAGEMENT

With the emergence of SOA, probably for the first time in computing, the capability exists to manage closely corporate business processes through tracking the underlying automation. It is now possible to align the execution of various individual SOA services, making up a business service directly with business indicators for that service. This advance in monitoring that collects vast amounts of data allows it to arrive at

 DATA THAT IS SUBJECTED TO REGULATORY PROCESSES HAS TO BE PROTECTED FROM ANY INTERVENTION SO THAT IT IS STABLE, RELIABLE AND RELEVANT TO PARTICULAR EVENTS. ""

timely decisions on the allocation of resources to support business processes. A business activity may be overloading the capacity of a downstream process. For example, an order-taking system may be taking in more orders than it can process. This results in customer dissatisfaction and a reduction in goodwill. There exists a need to throttle back order taking. Real-time monitoring of critical activities such as these is important and is an important element of SOA.

SECURITY OF SOA SYSTEMS MANAGEMENT

Earlier it was stated that various industry governance agencies increasingly turn to SOA to put in place standard and consistent communications between regulated companies and themselves. Thus, we find that SOA services have to offer a reliable and trusted provision of regulatory data. The regulatory organization has to be positively assured that, at any given moment, when data is required it is available. Data that is subjected to regulatory processes has to be protected from any intervention so that it is stable, reliable and relevant to

> There is a need for proactive tracking and, if necessary, intervention or **» SOA SECRET**
> request for intervention in order to maintain the expected service level. This meticulous attention and readiness to act require broad-based monitoring and instantaneous correlation of collected data, creating yet another requirement for substantial computing and data management capacity.

particular events. For example, non-interference with data is critical for FDA regulations. There has to be a high level of confidence that clinical results are accurately recorded and published and have not been altered by some malicious sources. Public safety, especially air traffic safety, requires not only the assurance that no one has tampered with the data but that all data have been recorded. All relevant information must be collected, secured and available when the agency demands it. The need to ensure the safety and the security of the data calls for an increased level of integrity and security of the (systems management) applications that manage it. This establishes the requirement that the computing platform used to manage regulated data and the SOA systems publishing it must be as secure, and likely more secure, than the computing environment actually processing that data.

THE CASE FOR A NEW SYSTEMS MANAGEMENT PLATFORM

The fundamental concept that we attempted to establish earlier, is that within a collection of servers making up the SOA systems, one (the systems management) server is always called upon in emergencies. When a failure occurs or an unexpected large volume of new requests arrives, demanding the provision of new capacity, this server must be there to manage the activities. Thus, the systems management platform is among those, or perhaps the one, which requires the highest availability.

So, given the high demands described in this chapter, which platform is best to serve as an SOA management hub? The answer, of course, depends on a company's specific needs. But one option that deserves serious consideration is the venerable mainframe. The mainframe has built a reputation as an industrial-strength platform for traditional, core business workloads. Having been fitted with the appropriate hardware and software technology, today's System z is more than able to meet the complex requirements of the SOA management hub.

Dr. George M. Galambos is an IBM Fellow and chief technology officer for IGS Canada. He has spent 31 years in information processing as a systems engineer and architect, focusing on high performance, high availability systems and networks, with emphasis on quantitative methods. He performed assignments in management consulting on IS issues, project reviews and risk assessment, evaluation of new opportunities, creating strategic IT plans. He co-developed IBM's end-to-end System Design Method, initiated IGS' SOA/Web Services strategy and the Services-Oriented Architecture and Method technique. He contributed to the identification and classification of common e-business problems and their solutions, leading to the formation of Patterns for e-business and the ESS Reference Architectures. The work on patterns served as a basis for a recently published book of same title. Dr. Galambos' current work is focused on SOA-based design, both in theory and in practice with IGS clients, on assets and their reuse as well as on strengthening the role of technology in IGS' business. In addition, he is a member of the IBM Academy of Technology.

[1]By SOA system in this context we refer to major application systems built by composition from SOA services where the system itself incorporates the invoking and invoked service implementations

[2]Admittedly, a plausible and desirable way of ensuring the qualities described above is to reduce the number of components in the first place. In other words, a better and more manageable option would be to have a single management domain, but that is not always possible or practical.

Chapter

7

THE SECURE, RESILIENT BUSINESS SYSTEM: A BALANCING ACT

An investment in service-oriented architecture must be matched by
the right investments in security and business continuity.
That's not as easy as it might sound.

BY BILL O'DONNELL

SOA improves business performance, but the nature of its openness
can raise new security issues. Therein lies the paradox. In this chapter,
I'll explain how companies can adopt SOA and maintain security—
without impeding the benefits of SOA.

The fact is, business applications are governed by a set of functional and
non-functional requirements. Functional requirements are an application's
business tasks. Examples of these are displaying customer account information and transferring funds between accounts. Functional requirements
are easy to identify and monitor. When a problem occurs, it's usually simple
to isolate and fix. An application's non-functional requirements (NFRs) do
not directly relate to a business task, but rather they define the "qualities"
with which that function will be endowed.

An application's NFRs would include performance, availability and security. NFRs can be difficult to isolate and monitor, because they usually

> ## THE NEED TO ENHANCE AND EXTEND SECURITY PROTECTION IS ONE IMPORTANT MANNER IN WHICH SOA DISRUPTS IT OPERATIONS.

reside within the interactions between the application and its operating platform. Some NFRs, such as performance, lend themselves to monitoring and assessment; others present a more serious management challenge.

This chapter focuses on two NFRs, security and business resilience. Both of them are critical to a successful SOA implementation, tend to be difficult to manage and illustrate distinct differences in how a loosely coupled distributed and a tightly coupled centralized infrastructure manage SOA.

When a company commits to SOA, it has to open its mission critical systems to the Internet. These systems have traditionally been kept under close guard and companies may not have the technologies or processes in place to expose them safely. Consequently, risk exposure will increase and require the adoption of enhanced security measures. The need to enhance and extend security protection is one important manner in which SOA disrupts IT operations.

A company's resiliency depends on the business risk it is willing to embrace and the correlation of that risk with IT infrastructure so that proper technologies and processes are available for the continuity of

A commitment to SOA requires all contributing enterprises to expand and tighten both their security environments and resiliency and continuity strategies.   » SOA SECRET

business operations. The concept of resiliency is best understood at either an organization with self-contained assets and processes or at enterprises that do not have SOA and thereby have a more clearly defined risk posture.

The adoption of SOA tends to obscure this defined portrait of risk. It functions by integrating both online and offline business processes. All of this requires a new way of thinking about risk and resiliency. For example, components for the development, marketing and sales systems may be integrated into a new SOA business process. When these systems were autonomous, a failure would only impact the continuity of one department. With an SOA business process, this same failure has enterprise-wide implications. In another example, an SOA business process may contain components from two distinct businesses. In this case, resiliency and business continuity will depend on services beyond the control of either company. This could have catastrophic results if mission critical services are involved. A commitment to SOA requires all contributing enterprises to expand and tighten both their security environments and resiliency and continuity strategies.

SECURING THE ENTERPRISE

A company contemplating IT security looks to firewalls, antivirus and spyware software and detection devices for protection. However, even with a combination of these technologies, most still feel uncertain and exposed. All realize that a security breach can not only cause pain to customers but often leads to negative publicity that can impact a business's reputation and hurt bottom line profitability.

A company that utilizes the Internet using a web browser can construct an acceptable security perimeter using a combination of technologies. However, when this same company commits to SOA, it may open and extend its borders to anonymous entities across the Internet. This introduces a new brand of risk. Many of the origins of

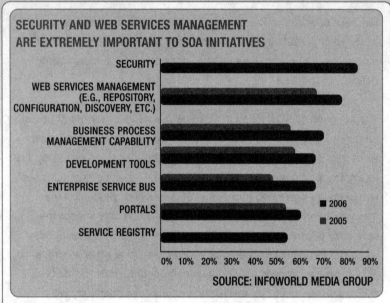

SECURITY AND WEB SERVICES MANAGEMENT
ARE EXTREMELY IMPORTANT TO SOA INITIATIVES

SOURCE: INFOWORLD MEDIA GROUP

components used in an end-to-end SOA business service are not under the company's control or even identified. Since the security profile of each application accessed by an SOA service is often unknown, the situation will likely arise where a business may not know much about either the specific service accessing its business application or the client using the business service that is driving the request.

New access points to mission critical systems can be open to service requests from the Internet and therefore subject to various risks. Adding to this problem, applications that use the Internet follow a client-server model where the client, like a web browser, connects to either middleware servers or directly to mission critical systems. Security implementations that work for this model with defined borders will not provide enough security enforcement in an SOA-driven, application-to-application model that shares components without borders. Total, system-wide security must be enhanced.

Obviously, SOA services demand a radically different security implementation. It requires an infrastructure that can maintain the security of systems that support, and applications that construct, a service in a manner that still enables Internet access. Without this, a company's risk profile becomes much more severe. Securing an SOA environment is difficult and less direct than securing a more traditional client-to-server environment. A number of traditional security concepts and technologies, such as intrusion detection, privacy aspect of data protection, identity management, auditability, regulatory compliance, virus protection and cryptography must be extended and enhanced.

Intrusion Detection. Intrusion detection technology combats unauthorized network intrusions such as malicious worms and ebusiness application "hacker" attacks. Effective intrusion detection technology immediately detects malicious activity and promptly notifies the organization of its presence. It's an important ingredient in securing most companies, especially those with an SOA implementation. Any intrusion that impacts a company's applications also infects other companies using that application as part of an SOA service. So not only can the infected company lose critical information and potentially confidential data, but so could each of the companies that use its applications. Currently, intrusion detection technologies assume a client-to-server connection. This technology must be enhanced to drill down to the application level to detect an intrusion within SOA-defined access points.

Privacy. Organizations are ultimately responsible for protecting customer privileged information. Hence, companies must be proactive in protecting this information from malicious use not only from unautho-

A company that utilizes the Internet using a web browser can construct an » **SOA SECRET** **acceptable security perimeter using a combination of technologies. However, when this same company commits to SOA, it may open and extend its borders to anonymous entities across the Internet.**

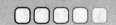

> ## SECURING AN SOA ENVIRONMENT IS DIFFICULT AND LESS DIRECT THAN SECURING A MORE TRADITIONAL CLIENT-TO-SERVER ENVIRONMENT.

rized network access, but also from internal staff without a need to know. Identity thieves simply need a name, Social Security number and a birth date to steal identity successfully. Effective SOA application-to-application sharing will depend on the infrastructure's ability to create and maintain the security of this information.

Identity Management. Identity management technologies manage the information used to prove an individual's identity. This is often in the form of user IDs or email addresses and passwords. These technologies can dynamically manage access control to specific applications and data. However, for an SOA service this capability needs to be extended down to an application or service-component level that may be part of an SOA request. It also needs to manage the access of the end user driving the application service request.

Auditability. Audit reporting can be used to identify the source of unwanted events and as an ongoing gauge to measure the success of existing security efforts. A successful audit within an SOA deployment should include reports identifying who or what is accessing a company's network externally. This should include: the applications being accessed for an SOA service and the end user driving that request; the functions being driven within an SOA application; and all access to internal data.

Auditing must also include the identity of the driving entity accessing the data and how the data has been changed. In the likely event of an unauthorized access attempt, whether successful or not, it is necessary to register and classify that effort. Auditing capabilities need to be expanded to envelope the increased exposure of a company's system affected by an SOA implementation. A company with SOA requires strict auditing especially if conducting any business-to-business exchanges with companies whose security profile is unknown. Auditability is central to an SOA implementation.

Regulation and Compliance. Organizations understand the need to be fully aware of any security, regulatory and/or compliance requirements that impact them, their business partners and customers. SOA services that instigate data exchange need additional vigilance. For example, in the health industry, HIPPA may have some additional requirements if critical data is being exchanged between SOA services.

Virus protection. Virus attacks are a common occurrence. Often a measure to minimize these attacks is to quarantine infected systems. An effective quarantine could either inhibit an SOA service or more seriously infect it and deliver the virus to other companies. Therefore, special attention is required when mission critical and/or privacy information is being shared.

Cryptography. Cryptography technology is used to transfer sensitive information (such as Social Security numbers) securely across the Internet. It is utilized to accept credit cards or display personal account information. Many companies without SOA services have mature implementations of this technology. When adopting SOA, organizations need to consider implementing technology with

> **In order to construct an acceptable security profile, a distributed system** ⊗ **SOA SECRET** requires a set of application "moving parts" that each company must certify. If any one of these moving parts fails, the whole solution is in danger of failing.

improved protection of cryptography keys. The most secure implementation is hardware infrastructure that generates, manages and
protects cryptography keys in a manner that keeps this information
secret even from the administrator. Many banks currently use this
type of technology.

SOA services describe a volatile environment that encompasses a
constantly changing configuration of "n" systems, many of which are
unknown. This demands a new approach to security. Effective security
in this environment requires both strong technology and comprehensive, adroit governance.

SECURITY TECHNOLOGY

System security depends on minimizing vulnerabilities at each level. It
is futile to secure completely an operating system without applying similar efforts to the hardware and middleware layers. Security policy
implementation is simplified when these layers are integrated.
Integrated, centralized systems —mainframes — provide a seamless
exchange in problem determination and reporting so that event-driven
security issues can be easily identified and mitigated. This is a major
reason why integrated, centralized systems provide a solid wall of
security. The vendors of these systems control the construction of the
hardware and software layers and therefore present an integrated and
tested environment to applications.

The ability to protect the unknown is an important strength in mainframe
design. A mainframe's security originates at the hardware level with features that separate programs. The operating system exploits these features and provides a layer of protection that an application can't exploit.
Therefore, a poorly written application will not be able to overrun or take
over any aspect of the operating system or hardware. This design allows
a heterogeneous set of applications to run within the same system while
maintaining a secure layer of protection from internal or external attacks.
This is a critical element for an effective SOA deployment.

In contrast, the security profile of an SOA deployment in a distributed configuration can be difficult to manage and may result in a company's increased risk exposure. In a typical distributed system, many servers and software solutions may need to be introduced to achieve the required level of security along with a corresponding amount of planning, design and implementation. In addition, a company will have to assume responsibility for purchasing all appropriate security add-ons, as well as integrating them throughout the entire system since typically no single security vendor will provide the security solution for the entire configuration.

Adding to this complexity is the fact that not all combinations of security products have been previously tested together. This can add to a company's risk exposure. Therefore, in order to construct an acceptable security profile, a distributed system would require a set of application "moving parts" that each company must certify. If any one of these moving parts fails, the whole solution is in danger of failing. Moreover, even with an effective integration of these "parts," the configuration may become very complex and difficult to manage. This can confound problem determination efforts and negatively impact timely resolution.

SECURITY GOVERNANCE

Exposing mission critical systems to the Internet requires a very high level of governance regardless of the deployment platform. The centralized server has evolved with a built-in set of checks and balances that protect the environment from both external and internal attacks. It offers a consolidated infrastructure that can improve enterprise-

With SOA opening mission-critical systems to the Internet, it is imperative that its services reside on a resilient, fault-tolerant system that is available 24x7x365.

» **SOA SECRET**

 IT IS FUTILE TO SECURE COMPLETELY AN OPERATING SYSTEM WITHOUT APPLYING SIMILAR EFFORTS TO THE HARDWARE AND MIDDLEWARE LAYERS. **"**

wide security management. This is not possible with a more complex distributed server configuration.

For example, within a distributed system, a particular virus can only be neutralized after it has been discovered. In the meantime, the virus will infect all SOA services dependent on that system. With a configuration consisting of a multitude of servers, a virus can pose a serious problem since every server would need to be updated with new anti-virus configuration files. A virus infection on the mainframe is rare since the mainframe is designed to protect itself from virus intrusion. The security management solution prevents unauthorized users from circumventing or disabling any protection mechanisms in the system.

MAINTAINING BUSINESS CONTINUITY

An organization now must operate at the convenience of its customers. Therefore, its SOA service may be accessed on a weekend or at 2 a.m. If those services are not available, business will be negatively impacted. With SOA opening mission-critical systems to the Internet, it is imperative that its services reside on a resilient, fault-tolerant system that is available 24x7x365.

An important component of an organization's resilience is continuity of operations. When an organization suffers a catastrophe that impacts its IT, the most important requirements for a speedy recovery are the security of its information, the continuous availability of its systems and the implementation of a near-transparent disaster recovery plan.

Resiliency is even more important for SOA since the end-to-end transaction flow of SOA services can cross a number of systems.

A non-SOA service could go down and not impact any other service. In contrast, an SOA service may be a composite of services from several different external partners, so this same outage for an SOA service at one company could mean an outage for several companies. The availability of an SOA service is a product of the availability of each system that contributes a component. So, if the service uses components from four different systems, and each system is 99% available, than the availability of that specific service is a product of all four system availabilities (0.99 x 0.99 x 0.99 x .99 or 96%).

Therefore, as SOA services draw from a growing number of systems, the availability of that service has a growing dependence on the availability of each system. Certain technologies will allow an SOA infrastructure to continue operations 24x7x365 even when unexpected events occur. These technologies can accommodate a wide range of disaster scenarios from small, unplanned events though a major disaster and maintain a seamless and continuous business operation.

A disaster recovery effort can easily become a company catastrophe if its mission critical services can't be reconstructed. In a decentralized system, an enterprise-wide business process may have critical information scattered across desktops, servers and the mainframe. The business process can't continue until every element is fully recovered

Certain technologies will allow an SOA infrastructure to continue operations 24x7x365 even when unexpected events occur. These technologies can accommodate a wide range of disaster scenarios from small, unplanned events though a major disaster and maintain a seamless and continuous business operation. » **SOA SECRET**

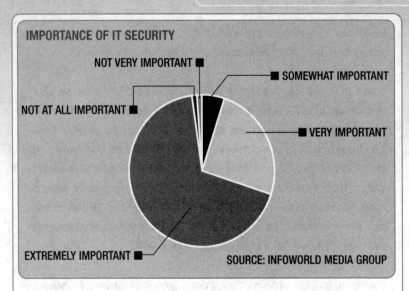

IMPORTANCE OF IT SECURITY

NOT VERY IMPORTANT ■

■ SOMEWHAT IMPORTANT

NOT AT ALL IMPORTANT ■

■ VERY IMPORTANT

EXTREMELY IMPORTANT ■

SOURCE: INFOWORLD MEDIA GROUP

and even then it may be ineffective if restoration to the exact point in time of the failure is not enacted. Recovering all of this information may be nearly impossible, and restoring it would take Herculean efforts since an entire backup for each system would have to be available. Moreover, coordinating all of these backups to the exact point of failure is a near impossible task.

Any enterprise incorporating SOA technologies must put together a comprehensive business resilience plan. These elements are fundamentals for a successful plan:

» Integrated risk management. Clearly identify operational business risks and the technology to respond and best manage those risks.

» Continuity of business operations. Identify and maintain a business continuity plan in the event of an outage. The plan must include the business processes and infrastructures that must respond in the event of a outage or disaster.

» Regulatory compliance. Document and ensure that the business complies with current government and industry regulations and standards, especially regarding the integrity and availability of information.

» Security, privacy and data protection. Ensure the security and privacy of data, information, systems and people with the right policies, methods, tools and overall governance.

» Knowledge, expertise and skills. Address resiliency by assuring that the right resources are in the right place and will be available at the right time.

» Market readiness. Enhance the company's ability to sense and respond to shifting customer demands and new market opportunities.

TO CENTRALIZE OR DECENTRALIZE

There were numerous reasons why organizations moved from their historically centralized server configuration to a decentralized network of servers. However, as the server farms supporting these organizations grew, an unintended degree of complexity was introduced. Now, when one server within a large decentralized network experiences a failure, determining the source of the problem can be extremely difficult. An SOA deployment can make any local server outage have system-wide, even cross-company implications. For example, if there were a burning smell in the computer room with 1,000 servers and no visible signs of fire, how long would it take to isolate the origins of that smell?

Centralized servers provide a range of resiliency options. They can back up and restore from a number of geographically separated datacenters and maintain the ability to continue to operate even if one datacenter is impacted by a major disaster. For example, a company can have a datacenter in Dallas and a datacenter in New York and, if the Dallas center went down, the SOA service would seamlessly transfer to New York and continue to operate as if nothing had occurred. This offers a company more manageable control in conducting an end-to-end business recovery.

One recurring argument against a centralized server is that it provides a single point of failure for the enterprise. This argument appears plau-

sible considering the total organizational dependence on one "box." However, there are two things to consider. First, the mainframe and its key external devices, like storage, have achieved mean time between failure (MTBF) ratings measured in decades. Second, an additional box or two can easily be added to construct a tightly coupled cluster configuration that enables a "virtual box" to span geographically. This design would endure a full datacenter outage in one location without disrupting enterprise-wide SOA service; and in the absence of an outage, all installed capacity is available for production work (i.e., it is not necessary to provision servers that only perform meaningful work when a failure occurs).

In conclusion, SOA technologies provide a company with a great degree of flexibility in building services to meet functional component requirements. A compelling aspect of SOA is that it is platform-agnostic. The business behavior of a service will be functionally identical regardless of the platform on which it is deployed. However, the ability for a service to meet an organization's non-functional requirements is directly tied to the quality of the underlying platform. In both security and business resiliency, a centralized server offers a superior solution. It tends to be more secure, fault-tolerant and resilient then distributed solutions. It is also much less complex, which simplifies the deployment and management of SOA.

Bill O'Donnell is a former owner of OAS Software Consulting who recently joined IBM's WebSphere Application Server Development organization, specializing in security. He has more than 20 years of experience in both technical support and application development on z/OS and distributed platforms and eight years in the development and exploitation of Java on the z/OS platform. He currently is a member of IBM's leadership council, co-chairing the Security Working Group, and is active in many of the company's SOA working groups.

Chapter

8

BIG IRON/LITTLE IRON

Deciding on the proper platform[s] and ways to scale resources within
an SOA project can be daunting. But it can be done. The key is to know
when resources should be shared and how to reconfigure management
systems to make it all work.

BY RORY CANELLIS & JOSEPH TEMPLE

Service-oriented architecture is platform neutral. Applications can be
developed without regard to the target system on which they will ultimately run. Its benefits can accrue to all systems when they are properly developed and deployed. However, this platform neutrality has tended
to promote SOA deployments that are distributed in nature, thus potentially
increasing communications traffic by adding strain to a topology, especially
one that expands horizontally. This chapter explores how various platform
types handle SOA, especially in an expanding environment.

ARCHITECTURES FOR CLUSTERING

The three architectures that enable a system to expand to meet growing
requirements fall under different types: those that scale up; those that scale
out; and, finally, those that combine both approaches.

Scaling Up/Scaling Out

Increasing system capacity by scaling up simply requires that the existing
computer system be made bigger. This is not clustering, but rather it

THE NEED TO SCALE OUT CAN BE DRIVEN EITHER BY THE ADDITION OF A SPECIFIC APPLICATION OR BY THE COMPOSITE GROWTH OF A WORKLOAD. IN A DISTRIBUTED WORLD, IT'S USUALLY THE FIRST CASE. IN A CENTRALIZED ENVIRONMENT, IT'S OFTEN THE SECOND.

increases the capacity of an individual system. In the past, when a company needed more capacity, it simply bought a bigger computer. A similar event occurs today when a company adds processors to its existing machine or upgrades to the next generation of systems. That's the idea of scale up: when more capacity is needed, it's added within the same machine or by replacing the existing machine.

Increasing system capacity by scaling out is accomplished by adding new machines to a configuration. A configuration with three machines will receive added capacity by adding a fourth machine. Simple, right? By scaling out, the granularity of system growth is the size of the added machine. By scaling up, the granularity of system growth can be quite small, even to the point of eventually adding capacity simply by changing a machine's microcode.

For example, in a four-way System z mainframe, a microcode change can add as few as one partial to as many as three more engines. Even though this may be a large change, it's not on the scale of adding a whole machine. A machine with the sophistication of the System z can also allow the user to turn on additional processors temporarily (known as Capacity Up/Down On Demand or CUDoD). This provides a type of flexibility generally unattainable in a scale out solution.

The need to scale out can be driven either by the addition of a specific application or by the composite growth of a workload. In a distributed world, it's usually the first case. In a centralized environment, it's often the second. When running a mixed workload on a centralized system, the composite load is the concern, even though one or two applications may drive a specific increase in capacity demand. In distributed processing, the growth of a particular application is important because that's often the only application on a machine. Scale out solutions are best for applications that need a large amount of computer power, that can run in parallel. Many small parts of the job can be sent to different systems over the network and then the results can be gathered for final integration.

One problem with scale out is that existing resources are never totally utilized. Work is assigned to a particular server, and it's impossible to balance this work allocation perfectly. Another potential problem in a scale out architecture is the speed of the communication pipeline carrying data from one processor in the cluster to another.

The result of this inefficient work allocation and communication speed is that a total scaled out system can simultaneously have both over-utilized and under-utilized servers. At the extreme, server A can be totally overwhelmed while server C is completely unused. In many cases, the composite utilization of scale out networks is very low. By contrast, a centralized system, which is designed and built to share

It is important to understand that for any type of system, distributing ⚫ **SOA SECRET** resources leads to a need for greater head room to meet a given service level. This is true whether the resources in question are servers, processors, memory, cache, warehouses, airports, factory work stations or business systems. Consequently, scale out solutions will generally run at lower utilization than scale up solutions.

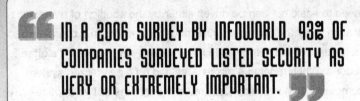

> ## IN A 2006 SURVEY BY INFOWORLD, 93% OF COMPANIES SURVEYED LISTED SECURITY AS VERY OR EXTREMELY IMPORTANT.

workload, often runs at much higher utilization rates. Many of them can be overcommitted at a particular point in time and run at 100% utilization to address the highest priorities of the organization, while deferring work with low priority for a later time. That's a major contrast between scale up and scale out. In essence, scaling up encourages the sharing of resources, while scaling out does not. It is important to understand that for any type of system, distributing resources leads to a need for greater head room to meet a given service level. This is true whether the resources in question are servers, processors, memory, cache, warehouses, airports, factory work stations or business systems. Consequently, scale out solutions will generally run at lower utilization than scale up solutions.

Scaling Up and Out in a Different Manner

A scale out cluster, as typically implemented, does not easily share resources. A degree of data sharing can be accomplished by the addition of software, such as a shared file system or a database designed to run on a cluster. However, these implementations can be expensive and complex to manage. In contrast, a scale up and out architecture (as exemplified by the System z Parallel Sysplex) is a shared environment. Work is moved around this Sysplex configuration in a more dynamic fashion because it was designed from its inception to share all data connected with it. Also, instead of just having one machine's worth of resources and data, it includes additional resources and data with some added hardware that allows data residing on storage farms to be shared dynamically. This enables configurations to be scaled up to new models as new physical capacity is added. That's unique.

With most clustered systems, customers pick the component parts needed to scale out and assemble a kit. The systems and communications methodologies are generally chosen separately. It's then up to the people putting these systems together to make all implementation decisions. With a centralized Parallel Sysplex system, all of these components are designed to work together. It's built to be adaptive so it can manage a wide variety of different kinds of work, and its integrated design can rebalance resources across workloads more easily.

The Case of Mixed Platform Scaling

Another common clustering architecture scales up and scales out within a mixed architecture. Most companies have applications that already exist on other platforms. A major factor contributing to this is that many multi-tiered applications were purchased in the 1999-2000 timeframe in response to Y2K. Companies replaced their proprietary business applications with packages like SAP, Siebel and PeopleSoft. These applications did not run on the mainframe, but rather, with it. The database resides on the mainframe, but the actual application runs on a distributed server. While most of these packages come in versions where the the database and application code can run on the same server, such servers — usually UNIX boxes — generally cannot scale large enough to handle both functions for high volume installations. In addition, the mainframe provides a high degree of security for the repository of information that hackers most want to steal. In a 2006 survey by *InfoWorld*, 93% of companies surveyed listed security as very or extremely important. The mainframe is noted for its security.

> **Some companies would like to combine the big iron data vault and** » **SOA SECRET**
> **smaller application servers. A layer of management software that can successfully coordinate these two is important to SOA. The Tivoli software suite provides the ability to combine the management of "big iron" and "little iron."**

A second reason to configure in a mixed environment: the billions of dollars of code developed for, and still residing on, the mainframe. Companies want to reuse that code since it represents a huge investment in time and resources and is often critical to company operations. And they want to keep it on the mainframe. Conversely, many companies would prefer that the code developed on distributed servers be kept where it was created, but they also want to be able to reuse that code. Therefore, the need for security leads companies toward the mainframe.

Some companies would like to combine the big iron data vault and smaller application servers. A layer of management software that can successfully coordinate these two is important to SOA. The Tivoli software suite provides the ability to combine the management of "big iron" and "little iron." In an integrated solution with centralized and decentralized systems, a company gets one or multiple large systems that can be maintained in a single location, and with a single system image (such as IBM System z Parallel Sysplex) to maximize data protection and reuse its large investments in both mainframe-based code and the smaller boxes that allow the deployment of applications at an appropriate level. For example, presentation services can be deployed very efficiently on little iron for data drawn from the big server. This allows for an attractive and efficient graphical interface to present the data to the user.

ADVANTAGES AND DISADVANTAGES

One large virtual Parallel Sysplex can be developed within a single System z machine. This centralized system can both scale up and scale out. In a scale up environment it can scale out virtually, while in a scale out environment its dynamic sharing capability mirrors that of a scale up cluster. The difference is in dynamic resource sharing and work scheduling. The advantage of a centralized system is that it can be kept very busy. However, since it's not comprised of commodity components, it can initially be an expensive system to build, which is a disadvantage. The difference in price can be so large that a customer might be able to acquire enough scale out machines to get the same theoretical capacity as a centralized Sysplex. However, similar capacity does not mean that the scaled out system will get the same amount of work done.

Getting the Work Done

The biggest consideration for any system is its ability to get the work done. If the distributed system is not able to complete the necessary work within an acceptable time, then a centralized system is obviously the better choice. There is something to be said for both distributed and centralized configurations. Customers with centralized systems, like Sysplex, have to buy expensive hardware. Those who opt for the less expensive hardware of distributed systems need to increase system utilization and deploy more people and power to run their networks.

This need to increase system utilization has led to a flood of software that attempts to emulate mainframe capabilities in workload management, fail-over for high availability and virtualization that allows multiple solutions to share hardware, security and accounting. However, most of this software addresses only one of these functions, and the user is left to do the integration. Vendors of distributed systems and independent software vendors can and have identified almost all of these functions on a point-by-point basis and attempt to address them with software. The cost of these additional software "piece parts" is often not included in server price/performance calculations, hiding the real cost of a distributed solution. Scaling out a configuration by adding servers to a cluster can have significant costs. Each additional server brings additional demands, such as more floor space, higher utility costs for power and cooling, higher software costs and additional staffing requirements to manage an environment of growing complexity.

> **ADDING SO MUCH SOFTWARE OFTEN RESULTS IN PERFORMANCE THAT FALLS FAR SHORT OF THE BENCHMARK RATINGS OF THE MACHINES. THE OVERHEAD REQUIRED BY EACH APPLICATION, WHICH IS GENERALLY NOT PRESENT WHEN THE BENCHMARKS WERE RUN, CONSUMES A SIGNIFICANT AMOUNT OF SERVER CAPACITY.**

Furthermore, controls that use feedback from the state of the system to automate operations, such as job handling and workload management, must be engineered by the end user since they are added on, rather than built into the system design. Inevitably, the controls are either less responsive or less stable than they are when integrated into the design of a shared system. In part this is due both to the overhead of sharing the engineering and the delay in the feedback paths inherent when the solution under control spans a network of distributed servers.

Performance Degradations

Adding so much software often results in performance that falls short of the benchmark ratings of the machines. The overhead required by each application, which is generally not present when the benchmarks were run, consumes a significant amount of server capacity. A centralized system may have the same overhead, but some of that overhead is handled by firmware within the system. In the IBM System z, this firmware is always present so that there is far less degradation from benchmarked results in a workload-managed, highly available environment with security and accounting.

Also in a centralized system, particularly for database applications, having the database manager residing in a single place means less communication traffic. For example, the communications required in a distributed environment to access high volume data controlled by a database lock manager that resides on one node of a distributed system would be as follows:

1. The program running on node A needs to update data. It communicates with the lock manager resident on node B to gain access.

2. The lock manager communicates back to node A to deny access because the data is currently being updated by another node.

3. The lock manager then checks to see who is currently accessing this data. Node C is currently updating this data and blocking other access.

4. The lock manager then must ask node C if it's finished with the data yet.

5. Node C communicates back that it's finished.

6. Now the lock manager can release the data. It releases the lock, goes back to node A and tells it, ok, you can now update.

7. Then node A updates the data and goes back to the node manager to state that it's now unlocking the data.

All of this communication occurs over the network. This not only increases traffic, it also causes a major problem with scalability.

In addition, in a clustered or distributed environment, overhead is often repeated in each server added to the cluster. In a distributed

> **SOA SECRET**

Vendors of distributed systems and independent software vendors can and have identified almost all of these functions on a point-by-point basis and address them with software. The cost of these additional software "piece parts" is often not included in server price/performance calculations, hiding the real cost of distributed solution.

system, each entity has to have its own headroom. That is it must be configured for the peak load of its part of the work. In transactional business solutions, the load varies more randomly than in large analytic or numerically intense workloads. Thus the load is represented statistically as an average and a standard deviation:

$$Load = Load_{avg} + z\rho$$

Here, ρ is the standard deviation and z represents the number of deviations that covered by the service level. For example, when the load standard deviation is half the average and we want to cover 97% of the cases encountered, z is 2. If we want to cover 99.7% of the cases, then z is 3. When distributed loads are combined, the variance's square of the standard deviations are added. This can be illustrated by the combined load:

$$Load = N\,Load_{avg} + z\sqrt{N}\rho$$

If the work of one shared server is distributed over N new servers, the headroom required to meet a particular service level z grows by a factor of $\sqrt{N}$.

So, with two servers, headroom increases by 140%. The larger the number of servers, the greater the total amount of overhead needed. A larger amount of headroom required leads to lower utilization or to a less robust service level. This is inevitable and can only be mitigated by removing variability from the load. This is one reason why numerically intense and business analytics have been more readily moved to distributed environments than transactional business work.

Another issue occurs with system throughput. A distributed system is typically built with fast processors surrounded by inexpensive infrastructure. Therefore, when the workload puts pressure on the system, the processors respond, but the components that surround the processor, such as caches, memory and I/O channels, do not because of a dearth in bandwidth. In short, the communications bandwidth becomes a bottleneck. What then happens, throughput flattens out even as utilization goes higher. This is called saturation. Very often, distributed platforms in a scaled out architecture will saturate at much lower utilization than a centralized system. Scaling out also leads to additional delays for network communication, which exacerbates the problem. This leads to additional performance issues and variability in the relative system capacity.

Costs

Then there are costs, which are mostly hidden. A distributed system is based on inexpensive processors and inexpensive infrastructure. However, the cost savings on hardware is often shifted to software and networking. The software can be expensive and complex to manage. When considering a cluster and its attractively priced hardware, it's critical to keep in mind that something has to manage this hardware, and the software designed to do so can be very expensive. Software costs also tend to increase with the growth of the distributed system.

The result may be that as the system becomes ever larger, the hardware becomes more of a commodity but the necessary software becomes more complex and expensive. The complexity leads to increases in staffing costs, impacts availability and can lead to additional hardware requirements as the need for headroom grows, further generating more complexity. The power bills, staffing and space expenses all increase with the size of the configuration.

Availability

There is also a more subtle issue with availability. Oftentimes, clustering is used to increase availability by creating redundancy. A cluster that has reached a flattening of its throughput through saturation has dramatically less availability that it did before the servers saturate. When saturation occurs, more servers will be needed to be effectively

 IT'S NOT NECESSARILY TRUE THAT ADDING ANOTHER SERVER, OR SPLITTING WORK BETWEEN SEVERAL SERVERS, WILL RESULT IN THE REQUIRED AVAILABILITY. ""

redundant. For example, one application can run on a small machine at 70% to 80% utilization. To increase the availability of this application, a second server is added to run in parallel. The work will be distributed between them so each will be operated at about 40%. Now, if one of them fails, the total system will operate at about 80% utilization, which may be acceptable if the operating system is robust enough to handle such high utilization levels.

However, the assumption here is that the saturation curve is linear, meaning adding the work of a failed server operating at 40% will use only 40% of the server capacity that it rolls into. If that's not the case and the curve actually declines, adding the workload of a failed server operating at 40% will use more than 40% of the other server's capacity. Then effective availability is drastically reduced, because there is no longer redundancy at 40% utilization. Thus, in the face of saturation, either larger servers must run at lower utilization or server redundancy will be required to meet the load and availability requirement.

The problem is that solution designers often think that the redundancy requirement for high availability can be addressed simply with a redundant server, while what is frequently required is both a redundant server and redundant capacity. It's not necessarily true that adding another server, or splitting work between several servers, will result in the required availability. The saturation curve defines available capacity within a distributed system. So, a company running concurrent servers at low utilization may need still more servers to provide a high level of application availability. This will push utilization down and costs up.

Management

Vendors of distributed systems recognize the problem of low utilization and are developing solutions to address it. Some of these solutions include virtualization, grid computing and intelligent workload management. All of these technologies are included within their systems to increase utilization in a mixed workload environment. The expectation is that utilization rates will increase, making the system more efficient and able to take advantage of a centralized system. The problem is that every one of these technologies often requires management capabilities with almost real-time attention to monitor activity and comprehend the dynamics.

Unfortunately, the tools currently available for UNIX, Windows and Linux provide only limited capability to monitor and control these products. Management becomes even more difficult when these technologies to improve benchmark speed are incorporated into systems and interact with virtualization technology. For example, the IBM System p has a multi-threading technology (SMP) and micropartitioning virtualization. With those two environments running together, it's extremely difficult to ascertain utilization and, hence, makes it difficult

When considering a cluster and its attractively priced hardware, it's   » **SOA SECRET**
critical to keep in mind that something has to manage this hardware, and the software designed to do so can be very expensive. Software costs also tend to increase with the growth of the distributed system. The result may be that as the system becomes ever larger, the hardware becomes more of a commodity but the necessary software becomes more complex and expensive.

> THE ADVANTAGE OF A CENTRALIZED SYSTEM IS THAT IT CAN BE KEPT VERY BUSY. HOWEVER, SINCE IT'S UNIQUE AND NOT COMPRISED OF COMMODITY COMPONENTS, IT CAN INITIALLY BE AN EXPENSIVE SYSTEM TO BUILD, WHICH IS A DISADVANTAGE.

to manage. That's because utilization counters in the machines are based on processors. Therefore, it's hard to discern which thread of the multi-threading used a specific portion of the processor. It's also difficult to determine how much of the processor is actually being used.

The point is that management tools of distributed systems are primitive relative to System z, and the ability to understand and react to conditions like these hasn't been fully developed yet. Finally, multi-threading paradigms conflict with efforts to increase utilization, since they are designed to kick off many parallel computing threads from a common source. This conflicts with the concept of running many different things at the same time.

Monitoring and management on "distributed" systems face a four-fold challenge:

1. There is a need to increase system utilization.
2. The technologies for increasing multithreaded throughput are at odds with the technologies which enable increased utilization.
3. The tooling and fundamental instrumentation hasn't kept pace with the new technologies designed to increase throughput with multithreading and utilization with virtualization and workload management.
4. The basic designs of UNIX and Intel machines are optimized for

processing large programs with many threads, as opposed to processing many small programs that are sharing the resource. This design issue goes beyond the processor and the caching out to the I/O, as well.

SUMMARY

A systems hierarchy has begun to emerge. The System z is designed for resource sharing, as are, to a lesser extent, the large UNIX machines. Following these are systems in distributed environments that incorporate virtualization and conduct management across the entire network.

The more a system is scaled out, the more difficult and expensive it becomes to increase its utilization. The length of the feedback loop for discovering system imbalances and determining and implementing appropriate action — so essential in dynamic-sharing resources — also varies. The System z is hard-wired, so its feedback loop is minimized. When this loop is built on top of a Windows, Linux or UNIX operating system, it's not quite as effective because it's not built into the structure of the machine and operating system. Instead, it resides in the middleware. Within a large network, the feedback loop dependent on multiple system and network technologies and communication speeds is even longer.

An individual SOA service may behave like a single application or it may have many diverse users with various priorities, service usage profiles and peak/average loads. In some cases this will cause the

> **» SOA SECRET**
>
> The more a system is scaled out, the more difficult and expensive it becomes to increase its utilization. The length of the feedback loop for discovering system imbalances and determining and implementing appropriate action — so essential in dynamically sharing resources — also varies.

EVOLUTION OF THE PROCESSING APPLIANCE

By Dr. Gururaj Rao, IBM Fellow and Hardware Systems Chief Engineer, IBM Systems & Technology Group

Service-oriented architecture is driven by application and interface standardization. Historically, the business benefits of standardization are usually funded by a "tax" of ever-increasing processing cycles. This has been the case with XML, TCP/IP and the J2EE framework, for example. Fundamentally, standardization comes at a cost of processing and performance overhead. To accommodate this overhead, the industry trend is to develop special purpose systems that significantly improve the performance of these standardized services. For example, the system DataPower exists purely for processing XML and providing web services security.

Essentially, standards, especially in the context of SOA, require specialized functions that can be processed using various kinds of specialty technologies. For instance, cryptographic services can be implemented in a PCI card attached to the server. When this service is required, the card is given the task. This is transparent to the application and requires no change in application or middleware. A higher level of system-wide efficiency can be achieved by handing the work over to such specialty engines that are optimized for it. These engines can take the form of a processor card, part of a CPU or an entity external to the server box (often called an "appliance").

Two important industry trends have driven this move to specialty technology. For one, as SOA becomes more deeply entrenched, business processing will be increasingly more dependent on standards. Second is a drive towards software componentization as these business processes become implemented in a more or less modular way.

These trends in standardization and modularization require that specific functions become more efficient in their implementation. This can be accomplished by taking these functions either to a special engine, card, appliance or server that is optimized to do that function. When the specialty hardware is external to the server, a key part of this optimization process involves standards-based networking and associated high-performance network attachments, which allow peeling off that specific function, taking it elsewhere for processing and bringing it back with the lowest possible latency.

A third trend driving the emergence of specialty processing is the morphing of Moore's Law. The performance growth "predicted" in Moore's law can no longer be sustained on a single processing thread. However, throughput growth using a collection of smaller processing threads is sustainable. Thus, more and more tasks will be done in parallel via parallel threading. In a multi-threaded environment, specialty appliances or specialty processors can help to increase throughput beyond what's possible by using only a single thread as long as there is enough concurrency built into the application.

Much of the attention these days is on standalone specialty boxes, or appliances. The appliance model is very compelling because such boxes are relatively inexpensive, can be plugged into a configuration with little effort, and do a good job at reducing the standards-related overhead associated with SOA. However, the standalone form factor does have a downside in terms of increasing the number of physical boxes that need to be managed and driving additional consumption of electricity, cooling, floor space and related environmental concerns. Also, work that is offloaded to an appliance is temporarily removed from the workload management scope of the server processing the SOA service. None of these are significant issues in small or medium-size configurations, but as SOA services increase in scale, these considerations grow in importance.

At the other extreme from the standalone appliance model is the fully integrated specialty engine, as has been introduced into the IBM mainframes in recent years. A System z mainframe today offers the ability to designate server processors as specialty engines that are optimized to improve the throughput of particular workloads. The System z Application Assist Processor (zAAP) can be designated for execution of Java code; System z Integrated Information Processor (zIIP) for certain database functions; and Integrated Facility for Linux (IFL) for execution of the Linux operating system and associated applications.

One of the key distinguishing characteristics of this approach towards specialty processing is the fact that these internal engines are part of the shared memory multi-processor System z design. This allows computing capacity to be optimized for a particular environment while allowing the entire workload to fully participate in the workload management, scheduling, system management, recovery, security domains, etc., of the mainstream operating system. This is a significant advantage to having internal specialty engines.

Consider the zIIP as an example. A zIIP enables efficient handling of standards-based TCP/IP communications between remote application servers and System z database servers. Since the zIIP utilizes standards-based connectivity, the overhead of the standard is buried into the specialty engine processor. The result is highly efficient support in a standards-based environment that also affords the opportunity for conducting additional data processing functions on the System z. These internal specialty engines increase efficiency, especially in a standards environment and, because they are internal to the System z, do not incur the environmental overhead of standalone appliance boxes. Because these engines are integral to the mainframe operating environment, IT is relieved of the burden of configuring new boxes, conducting additional capacity planning exercises or worrying about how workload is going to get assigned.

To summarize, System z currently offers a variety of special internal engines that improve the efficiency of standards-based processing within the overall context of the mainframe operating environment. There is a parallel industry trend toward external appliances that are specialized for specific functions, driven by modularization, the standards matrix and easy provisioning of high-performance networking connectivity. Both approaches are aimed at making SOA processing more efficient.

Over time the goal is to bring all of these specialty processors into a more integrated and cohesive processing fabric so that they do not function as independent entities. All specialty processors — regardless of form factor — need to be tightly integrated together in order it increase their utility and allow SOA to be handled most efficiently.

service to be, by definition, a "mixed workload," requiring a higher bandwidth-to-CPU ratio moving the service into "Parallel Hell," the kind of problem that the mainframe's intended to solve. In another case, the usage of a particular SOA service may not justify a configuration of even minimum dedicated hardware. In such cases, the mainframe scale up solution will be a very attractive alternative to dedicating hardware to individual services.

Rory Canellis has spent 33 years in marketing and sales for large IBM systems in such areas as System z marketing; zSeries sales support; parallel computing (RS600 SP); visualization systems (RS6000); engineering and scientific computing; industrial sector applications; and systems engineering for mainframe accounts. She currently is Program Director for System z product differentiation, responsible for product analysis and differentiation of the System z from other platforms.

Joe Temple has been employed by IBM for the last 32 years, starting as a design engineer on 8100 "distributed processors" and later as a mainframe designer on the IBM 9121. He has since done work in advanced technology and product introduction of mainframes, product introduction and product engineering of the IBM RS6000 SP, and technology application engineering for IBM Micro Electronics. He currently works in technical sales support for the System z brand. He is an IBM Poughkeepsie Master inventor with over 25 U.S. patents. In April 2006, he was appointed an IBM Distinguished Engineer, primarily for on his work in analyzing and articulating the relative capacity of servers.

Chapter

⬡ ⬡ ⬡ 9 ⬡ ⬡ ⬡

THE ART OF 'VIRTUALIZING' RESOURCES

There's much that can be accomplished for an emerging class
of SOA applications, particularly using IBM's System z
mainframe virtualization technologies.

BY LES WYMAN

odern IT networks now are besieged with ever-growing demands.
This alone has increased the need to virtualize server footprints and
expand the workloads within emerging SOA environments that are
rapidly evolving in composition and processing requirements. The use of
historical static server capacity and provisioning disciplines becomes an
increasingly inefficient and expensive solution. Thus, a robust and efficient
server virtualization technology is needed to provide the capacity and flexibility required by this new environment.

Virtualization is the process of presenting a logical subset or superset of
physical computing resources to provide processing benefits beyond those
of the original configuration. It also refers to the process of presenting
computing resources for application use that may not physically exist, in a
manner that emulates the physical resources. An example would be "virtualizing" a storage device, such as a hard disk, by the transparent use of a
different physical resource, such as memory. This new *virtual* view of

> ## WITHIN ENTERPRISE-CLASS SERVERS, VIRTUALIZATION IS THE ABSTRACTION OF THE SERVER'S PHYSICAL RESOURCES, SUCH AS PROCESSORS, MEMORY, I/O INFRASTRUCTURE, ATTACHED DEVICES AND NETWORK CONNECTIONS.

resources is not restricted by implementation, geographic location or the physical configuration of the underlying resource. Commonly virtualized IT resources include computing power and data storage.

SERVER RESOURCE VIRTUALIZATION

Within enterprise-class servers, virtualization is the abstraction of the server's physical resources, such as processors, memory, I/O infrastructure, attached devices and network connections. It serves to provide multiple logical servers, typically called logical partitions or virtual machines, which operate on a common server footprint. These logical partitions or virtual machines are either subsets or supersets of various physical resources. They allow the concurrent and independent operation of multiple instances of operating systems, their associated subsystems and application software. The virtualization technology gives each such operating system "image" the appearance of having sole control over a distinct physical server and its resources. Abstractions like these can yield a substantial amount of IT consolidation and integration of both server hardware and software and overall IT management simplification. Virtualization also can significantly increase both the use and efficiency of a physical server by controlling and managing its otherwise unused physical resources. This becomes increasingly important for a successful SOA deployment environment. For example, it is necessary to accommodate the efficient exchange of information

between related workloads and to allow dynamic server resource
redistribution between such workloads.

WHY SERVERS ARE OFTEN UNDERUTILIZED

Reasons for server underutilization are numerous and complex.
However, they typically include both software's inability to scale and
an established, decentralized IT approach.

The Inability to Scale

Demands on software are increasing to meet growing company
requirements. But the operating systems, their subsystems and associated applications are often incapable of scaling effectively to utilize
the available physical server resources. The server hardware manufacturers, in contrast, are providing more robust servers that scale both
vertically with faster processors, memory and I/O and horizontally with
more SMP processors, memory and I/O — both at a rate greater than
can often be utilized by the resident software. This is epitomized with
the advent of CMOS hardware technologies that enable ever more
powerful, scalable and cost-effective computing platforms.

In many instances, software can't operate efficiently at the levels of
multiprogramming and/or multiprocessing necessary to support these
more scalable servers. This inability takes many forms, such as overly
serialized use of server resources, inadequate process threaded appli-

---

Many IT environments utilize a decentralized approach, characterized » SOA SECRET
by the deployment of one or two applications per
server. Typically done to either keep IT hardware costs
down or to localize server deployment to a specific
application or departmental goal, these segregated
server "farms" over time often expand to hundreds,
even thousands, of individual systems, each often
significantly underused.

cations and host operating systems with inadequate preemptive multi-programming or multiprocessing designs. These software inefficiencies have become increasingly commonplace with the use of open systems strategic programming models such as Java and XML at the application tier in the software stack. Although these programming models provide significant application development and deployment advantages in cost and time to market, by design, they distance the application developers from the "mechanics" of the physical platform on which their applications are deployed.

The Decentralized IT Approach

Many IT environments utilize a decentralized approach, characterized by the deployment of one or two applications per server. Typically done to either keep IT hardware costs down or to localize server deployment to a specific application or departmental goal, these segregated server "farms" over time often expand to hundreds, even thousands, of individual systems, each often significantly underused. It is common for servers in such a configuration to operate at 10 to 20 percent of their rated capacities. Furthermore, these distributed server environments often do not provide the network management and instrumentation metrics necessary to quantify and control this underutilization.

Many managers of distributed IT systems realize that their expanding server network is beginning to reach a size that inhibits an IT staff's ability to provide optimal assessment, control and management. Moreover, such configurations can significantly complicate overall network service and reliability. There is good reason, for example, why the Internet is classified as an unreliable network and requires extensive strategies, practices, overheads and redundancies to accommodate and minimize this unreliability. Implementing virtualization technologies that minimize the need for multiple servers can be justified in terms of simplifying IT infrastructure and reducing the cost of network ownership. Server virtualization, especially when deployed on a large, highly scalable enter-

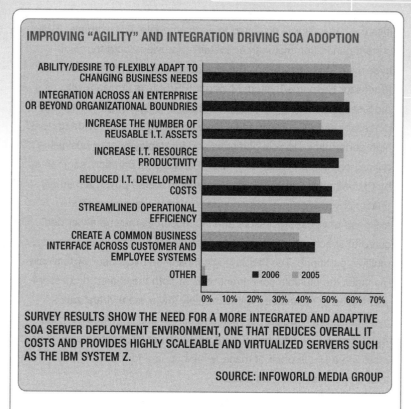

IMPROVING "AGILITY" AND INTEGRATION DRIVING SOA ADOPTION

(Bar chart comparing 2006 and 2005 survey results)

- ABILITY/DESIRE TO FLEXIBLY ADAPT TO CHANGING BUSINESS NEEDS
- INTEGRATION ACROSS AN ENTERPRISE OR BEYOND ORGANIZATIONAL BOUNDRIES
- INCREASE THE NUMBER OF REUSABLE I.T. ASSETS
- INCREASE I.T. RESOURCE PRODUCTIVITY
- REDUCED I.T. DEVELOPMENT COSTS
- STREAMLINED OPERATIONAL EFFICIENCY
- CREATE A COMMON BUSINESS INTERFACE ACROSS CUSTOMER AND EMPLOYEE SYSTEMS
- OTHER

■ 2006 ■ 2005

0% 10% 20% 30% 40% 50% 60% 70%

SURVEY RESULTS SHOW THE NEED FOR A MORE INTEGRATED AND ADAPTIVE SOA SERVER DEPLOYMENT ENVIRONMENT, ONE THAT REDUCES OVERALL IT COSTS AND PROVIDES HIGHLY SCALEABLE AND VIRTUALIZED SERVERS SUCH AS THE IBM SYSTEM Z.

SOURCE: INFOWORLD MEDIA GROUP

prise-class SMP server, can significantly reduce total network cost and simplify complexities inherent in distributed technologies.

SERVER VIRTUALIZATION

Two dominant forms of server virtualization, virtual machine support and logical partitioning, have evolved since the 1960s. Both forms abstract the physical server by creating multiple logical instances capable of operating both concurrently and independently on the same physical server. The technology component used to create and manage these capabilities is commonly called a hypervisor, which is typically implemented in both software and hardware form. In most instances, it operates between the server hardware and the operating system. Selection of a hypervisor virtualization technology is governed by the overall objectives and capabilities of the server and the capabil-

ities the hypervisor is designed to accommodate. For example, IBM's current generation mainframe, System z, provides both forms of hypervisor implementation. The logical partition implementation, Processor Resource/System Manager (PR/SM), is firmware with processor, memory and I/O infrastructure hardware logic, as well as processor and I/O infrastructure firmware designed to provide up to 60 high performance logical partitions and for deployment of business-critical, production-class workloads. Each logical partition, segmented by PR/SM, is assigned its own unique non-shared physical memory space, physical processors and associated I/O resources. The assigned physical processors and I/O resources may be either dedicated to specific partitions or transparently and dynamically shared by multiple partitions. The PR/SM logical partition hypervisor dynamically manages the multiple concurrent uses of both the shared processors and shared I/O resources with extremely low system virtualization overheads. Such logical partition and associated workload co-location significantly improves the efficient exchange of information as well as providing a single point of management control for the workloads and their typically shared data bases.

This level of virtualization enables System z processor utilization levels typically to reach well over 90 percent. PR/SM also provides other virtualization capabilities such as high-speed virtual LANs, called hipersockets, that allow software images to communicate across partitions at SMP memory speeds not seen on TCP/IP external networks operating at wire speeds. These communications can occur without the additional overhead typical within a physically distributed network. Physical network overhead such as data conversions, data compression/decompression and data encryption/decryption can be eliminated or minimized when communicating software images are deployed on the same secure, physical server platform.

A virtual machine hypervisor is the other dominant form of server virtualization. It enables the creation and deployment of multiple logical server instances called virtual machines. It supports similar processor and I/O virtualization capabilities as the logical partition hypervisor. With System z, the virtual machine hypervisor also provides virtualization capabilities and abstractions to accommodate very large numbers of virtual machine instances and provide a rich portfolio of functions designed to accommodate the concurrent development and testing of new applications and workloads on a single server.

The virtual machine hypervisor provided by System z with the z/VM operating system can consolidate underutilized physical servers and their applications. This is accomplished by employing finely grained memory virtualization that dynamically abstracts the server's physical memory into small physical memory "pages." These are then transparently assigned and shared by active virtual machine images. With the z/VM virtual machines hypervisor, the server's physical processors can be virtualized similarly to the PR/SM logical partition counterpart. It also can virtualize logical instances of server resources that do not physically exist. For example, it can create virtual processor instances and then transparently time-share their execution on a single processor which will create the illusion of a multiprocessor server. In addition, it can virtualize I/O devices (such as virtual disks) and networks (such as virtual LANs) in order to accommodate the software's processing, I/O and communications requirements. This type of network virtualization enhances the overall efficiencies and latencies of the virtual machine server network operating under the control of this hypervisor.

> **SOA SECRET**
>
> Because virtualization is relatively new for commodity servers and is provided by different hardware and software vendors, no one vendor is in control of the entire virtualized server footprint. However, with IBM's System z, the physical server architecture, hardware and software technologies are collectively designed by one company with virtualization as a fundamental requirement.

Such efficiencies are also possible with other I/O resource abstractions that are transparently mapped to physical server memory to accommodate the desired I/O virtualization. For example, the z/VM hypervisor also logically partitions physical disks into smaller mini-disks that can be concurrently allocated to different virtual machine instances to further utilize and share total disk space.

Emerging virtual machine hypervisors that support commodity servers, such as VMware and Xen, have not been generally deployed on large, scalable SMP servers. They are typically designed for and deployed on smaller two-, four- or eight-way servers. This is also true of the operating systems such as Windows, UNIX and Linux that typically support Intel-based servers. Consequently, the overall economy of scale and consolidation these servers can provide, even when virtualized, is yet to match that of a large enterprise-class server.

Because virtualization is relatively new for commodity servers and is provided by different hardware and software vendors, no one vendor is in control of the entire virtualized server footprint. However, with IBM's System z, the physical server architecture, hardware and software technologies are collectively designed by one company with virtualization as a fundamental requirement. The system's virtualization logic is always active and operating within the system even when only one software instance is deployed. These System z technologies are mature, robust, efficient, reliable and time-tested.

MEMORY VIRTUALIZATION

Server memory demands can increase exponentially when servicing SOA strategic programming models such as Java or XML. This creates even greater virtualization demands on the system's most heavily virtualized server resource: program-addressable random access memory (RAM). In RAM virtualization, a given physical memory of size x is virtualized to appear to programs as having the greater total capacity of $x+y$. The various forms of memory virtualization are typically provided

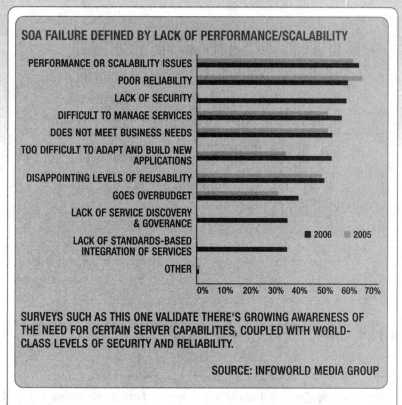

SOA FAILURE DEFINED BY LACK OF PERFORMANCE/SCALABILITY

SURVEYS SUCH AS THIS ONE VALIDATE THERE'S GROWING AWARENESS OF THE NEED FOR CERTAIN SERVER CAPABILITIES, COUPLED WITH WORLD-CLASS LEVELS OF SECURITY AND RELIABILITY.

SOURCE: INFOWORLD MEDIA GROUP

by a combination of server hardware and operating system software and support facilities.

System z provides two fundamental memory virtualization technologies:

1. Dynamic Address Translation (DAT). This is the basic virtual memory to physical memory address mapping technology. DAT hardware technology is exploited by the System z operating systems to provide multiple 64-bit virtual memory address spaces for use by each operating system instance. DAT hardware is further extended for use by the System z virtual machine hypervisor to allow deployment of large numbers of virtual machine instances operating within the z/VM logical partition.

2. Physical Memory Partitioning. This is a logical partition memory virtualization technology used by the PR/SM logical partition hypervi-

DEMANDS ON SOFTWARE ARE INCREASING TO MEET GROWING COMPANY REQUIREMENTS. BUT THE OPERATING SYSTEMS, THEIR SUBSYSTEMS AND ASSOCIATED APPLICATIONS ARE OFTEN INCAPABLE OF SCALING EFFECTIVELY TO UTILIZE THE AVAILABLE PHYSICAL SERVER RESOURCES. 99

sor to segment the server's program addressable physical memory into multiple logical memory spaces. Each of these is then assigned to a single logical partition instance.

EVALUATING MEMORY VIRTUALIZATION

Most server platforms provide some form of memory virtualization that is exploited by their respective operating systems or virtual machine technologies. These virtualizations, however, don't always match the functional robustness necessary to meet the SOA environment's demands. Correspondingly, this set of metrics should be used when evaluating memory virtualization:

Does memory virtualization technology provide partitioning and encapsulation of the servers' physical memory into multiple independent and logically partitioned address spaces that support high levels of security?

System z, for instance, provides for up to 60 high performance and secure logical partition address spaces, all of which are controlled by hardware-enforced address translation controls. These controls operate with no measurable memory access overhead and have achieved (Evaluation Assurance Level 5) security certification.

Does memory virtualization technology offer a large number of fine grained (e.g., 4K page size) memory virtualization and transparent sharing capabilities for both the operating systems and the virtual machine hypervisors?

Within each logical partition, System z provides for the dynamic creation of large numbers of virtual memory address spaces. Such spaces are exploited by both z/OS and System z Linux operating systems and their associated programming. For example, z/OS uses these virtual spaces to encapsulate and to protect various control program functions, subsystem functions such as WebSphere and DB2, and to insulate multiple independent application instances from each other. It also provides each such virtual instance with an almost unlimited supply of virtual memory. This is a necessity for memory-hungry SOA applications. The z/VM virtual machine hypervisor also exploits this technology to provide efficient creation and management of large numbers of virtual machine instances each of which may also exploit multiple virtual address spaces.

Does memory virtualization technology provide for the concurrent operation of multiple independent virtual memory address spaces?

System z allows multiple virtual memory address spaces to be concurrently active on the same physical processor. This enhances multi-programming and multi-processing of independent programming functions operating in separate virtual address spaces, as well as an efficient data exchange between applications and their associated subsystems while each operates in their own virtual memory space.

A virtual machine hypervisor is the other dominant form of server virtualization. It enables the creation and deployment of multiple logical server instances called virtual machines.

» **SOA SECRET**

The IBM system z PR/SM logical partitioning and z/VM virtual machine memory virtualization technologies are depicted in the following diagram.

FIGURE 1

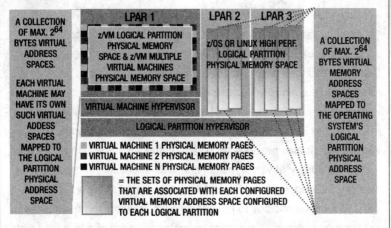

PROCESSOR VIRTUALIZATION

Virtualization technologies also provide various levels of processor abstraction. These range from assigning a dedicated subset of processors to a single logical partition, to the dynamic and transparent sharing of physical processors by multiple logical partitions or virtual machines. Shared process virtualization enables a more complete use of unused or "wasted" processor cycles or "white space" that can lead to increased processor utilizations and a reduced number of physical processors. Not all virtualization platforms provide the same degree of functional support for these processor virtualization derivatives. However, they all are based on the same virtualization principle: Using one or more levels of hardware, firmware and/or programming resources to accommodate the desired virtualization capabilities. In the case of System z, this means the creation of logical processor "state descriptions" that represent the configured physical processors, which are then assigned to a logical partition or virtual machine.

These "logical" processors contain the physical processor execution states and can be assigned to different logical partitions, or virtual machines, to form any multi-processor capacity, logical partition or virtual machine desired. This technology enables the physical processor resources to be dynamically and transparently shared, with a high degree of physical processor consumption granularity on a dynamically required or pre-defined basis. Figure 2 depicts an example of the System z processor virtualization capability.

FIGURE 2

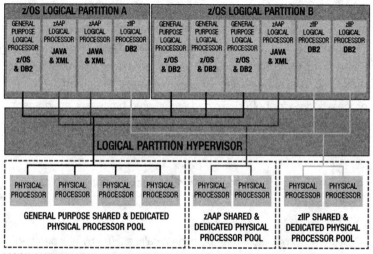

LOGICAL PARTITION HYPERVISOR: DISPATCHES LOGICAL PROCESSORS TO THEIR CORRESPONDING PHYSICAL PROCESSORS
zAAP (SYSTEM z APPLICATION ASSIST PROCESSOR) FOR EXECUTING JAVA INSTRUCTIONS
zIIP (SYSTEM z INTEGRATED INFORMATION PROCESSOR) FOR EXECUTING DB2 INSTRUCTIONS

EVALUATING PROCESSOR VIRTUALIZATION

Processor virtualization should be evaluated according to the following metrics:

Can the physical processors be virtualized and assigned as either dedicated to a partition or dynamically and transparently shared by multiple partitions or virtual machines?

Typically, physical processors are underutilized. However, they can be "multi-programmed" by a virtual machine hypervisor to accommodate multiple logical partitions and virtual machine instances, thereby improving physical processor utilization. The System z logical partitioning hypervisor provides both forms of processor virtualization. The PR/SM hypervisor maintains separate processor "pools" of each processor type for both dedicated and shared processor assignment. For the z/VM hypervisor, all physical processors configured to the z/VM logical partition are dynamically shared by all virtual machines.

How many logical partitions or virtual machines may share the processor?

All System z processors may be dynamically shared by all operating system instances with finely grained physical processor consumption for either logical partition or virtual machine encapsulations.

How well does physical processor utilization scale with shared multi-processor logical partitions or virtual machines?

Suboptimal processor sharing can result from inefficiencies in the processor virtualization controls within the hypervisor, the underlying physical processor hardware or the sharing operating systems instances. For example, inefficiency might occur when a logical processor executes on a physical processor and requires communication with another logical processor assigned to the same logical partition, but the other logical processor is currently inactive. The active logical processor may then be delayed in completing its task until the other logical processor is dispatched unless the hypervisor efficiently manages the situation. System z hypervisors and operating systems accommodate such possibilities and provide management strategies to minimize such shared processor multiprocessing effects.

Does the processor virtualization technology provide the ability to dynamically manage and regulate the amount of shared physical processor capacity each logical partition is permitted to consume?

System z hypervisors provide the monitoring and management of physical processor consumption by using dynamic workload management technologies. These technologies monitor and dynamically readjust processor consumption levels for each sharing logical partition or virtual machine to accommodate user-supplied workload goals and priorities.

How efficient is processor virtualization?

Unless the server's underlying hardware and associated infrastructures are designed to accommodate processor virtualization, significant processor capacity may be absorbed by the virtual machine hypervisor in order to accommodate processor virtualization and sharing. The greater this overhead, the greater is the potential of physical processor sharing to be compromised.

> **Shared process virtualization enables a more complete use of unused or**   » **SOA SECRET**
> **"wasted" processor cycles or "white space" that can lead to increased processor utilizations and a reduced number of physical processors.**

Again, using System z as an example, there's a complete set of low overhead processor virtualization controls to operate and share physical processors. Each processor provides all the controls necessary to accommodate all frequently executed synchronous operating system events (such as supervisor state instructions) and asynchronous events (such as timer interruptions or I/O interruptions) that would otherwise require hypervisor assistance. For example, frequently executed I/O instructions and I/O interruptions are executed by processor virtualization controls that allow these instructions and interruptions to "pass through" the hypervisor without its involvement (i.e., to operate on behalf of the logical partition or virtual machine software without hypervisor involvement).

Does processor virtualization require modifications to the software operating within the logical partitions or virtual machines?

Unless the processor virtualization controls are transparent to the various operating systems working within the logical partitions or virtual machines, the ability to deploy different versions of the platforms operating systems and associated applications may be impacted. With System z, processor virtualization controls are both transparent and compatible and accommodate the concurrent deployment of various operating system levels and their associated software stacks. This capability can be significant in providing concurrent deployment of both new SOA applications and legacy applications on the same physical server.

I/O RESOURCE VIRTUALIZATION

There are two I/O resource virtualization models used with the server's memory and processor virtualization controls to create and deploy logical partition and virtual machine instances. The first model partitions and assigns the server's physical I/O resources to one or more logical partitions or virtual machines. The second model creates and deploys virtualized I/O resources using a different resource, such as server memory, for assignment to logical partitions or virtual machines.

System z provides a full complement of I/O resource virtualization controls for both of these models. The partitioning model is exploited by the PR/SM hypervisor on behalf of the configured logical partitions. The second model is exploited by the z/VM hypervisor on behalf of the virtual machines it creates and controls.

The partitioning model provides the assignment and efficient use of server I/O channel paths and I/O adapters and the server's attached physical I/O resources. This partitioning technology also significantly increases the total number of I/O resources that may be configured to a System z mainframe to enable scaling of the server's I/O resources to its ever-expanding logical partitioning, processing and memory capacities. This technology allows the I/O resources to be either individually assigned to separate logical partitions or, more typically, to allow these resources to be concurrently, dynamically and transparently shared by multiple logical partitions. These attributes are becoming increasing fundamental to large-scale SOA deployment platforms.

The second virtualization model, as deployed by the z/VM operating system, provides a software level of I/O resource abstractions that offers increased virtualization and granularity. I/O resources such as channel paths, adapters and other attached I/O resources may be dynamically manufactured and deployed to virtual machine instances when no corresponding physical resource is configured. Additionally, it provides virtualizations for I/O resources that may no longer be supported by System z to provide compatibility for older operating system levels and their associated software stacks.

The z/VM hypervisor can create and deploy virtual disks, virtual consoles, virtual LANs and virtual LAN switches. It can emulate resources such as the Small Computer System Interface (SCSI) and Fixed Block

Architecture (FBA) disks. It can also logically partition physical disks into smaller mini-disks that provide capacity to multiple virtual machine instances. This can increase the use of the disk's physical capacity and reduce the total number of physical disks required.

Logical Partition I/O Resource Sharing

The System z I/O resource-sharing technology is called the Multiple Image Facility (MIF). When sharing I/O, each partition is assigned independent I/O resource descriptions or resource "images" that represent the physical I/O channel path or I/O adapter and its attached physical I/O resources to be shared by other partitions. Separate channel path and I/O adapter images (called channel path images), and I/O resource images (called subchannel images) are configured to each resource-sharing logical partition and are assigned a unique "logical partition identifier." These images contain the physical I/O control states necessary to access and operate the shared channel paths, adapters and the attached I/O resources of the sharing logical partition to which they are assigned. The system's asynchronous and free running channel paths and I/O adapters then use these respective channel path and subchannel images to "dispatch" and control the multiplexed execution of the I/O operations for the sharing operating system instances executing in their respective logical partitions.

This level of concurrent frame-multiplexed I/O execution control also links the logical partition identifier to the channel path's physical address. The logical address identifies the partition initiating the I/O operation through the link topology and at the I/O resource destination. Therefore, each I/O operation and associated I/O response event is tagged with the partition's logical address identifier. The shared channel path or adapter uses this identifier to select the appropriate image controls and logical partition memory space from which the I/O operation data transfers are to be made. It then reports the completion of the I/O operation to the appropriate logical partition without hypervisor intervention.

System z I/O resource-sharing technology is symmetrical. This means that the shared I/O resources at the other end of the I/O topology connecting the resource to the server can also provide this same level of resource-sharing. For example, the storage controllers used by System z provide a disk storage virtualization technology that allows the disk volumes to operate as multiple, concurrently accessible I/O resources. This disk-sharing capability is mutually exploited by both the storage controllers and operating systems to provide high levels of concurrent storage disk operations and I/O throughput. These System z and associated disk-storage I/O resource sharing capabilities are depicted in Figure 3.

FIGURE 3

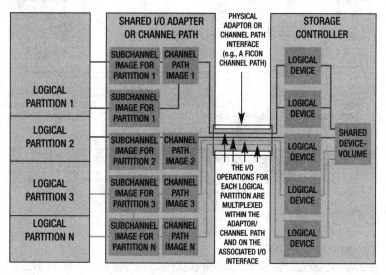

Logical Partition I/O Resource Scaling

The System z I/O resource scaling technology is called the Multiple Logical Channel Subsystem Facility (MLCS). It significantly increases System z channel subsystem and I/O resource capacities. This technology enables multiple software instances to take advantage of the mainframe's growing processing capacities and economies of scale. It

also enables System z to accommodate multiple channel subsystem instances which increase its total physical I/O capacity. Each such logical channel subsystem can be configured concurrently to multiple logical partitions. It also allows the System z logical partition I/O resource-sharing capability to accommodate all configured partitions regardless of the logical channel subsystem to which the partitions are configured as depicted in Figure 4.

FIGURE 4

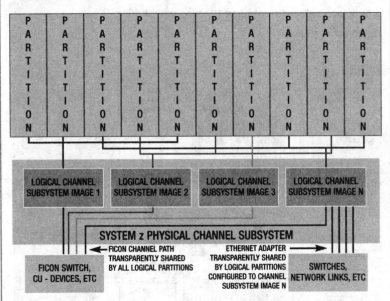

Evaluating I/O virtualization

Server I/O virtualization should be evaluated on the following metrics:

Can the server's I/O resources be partitioned and dedicated to a specific logical partition or virtual machine instance, and can resources be dynamically and transparently shared by multiple instances?

Partition-dedicated I/O resources are typically required when a logical partition either has robust I/O processing requirements or the partition is not permitted to share its I/O resources for security's sake. Although this capability is not applicable to many IT environments, it is an attribute the server's virtualization portfolio should provide. With System z, all of its I/O infrastructure and associated I/O resources may be configured as either dedicated to or shared by specific logical partitions.

Other server platforms may provide a level of I/O resource sharing by using software virtualization techniques. Their ability to provide efficient I/O resource sharing with low I/O virtualization overheads is still being developed. In contrast, System z currently provides I/O resource-sharing capabilities with less than 1% overhead. This technology has been available since the early 1990s and it can significantly improve the overall throughput of both the I/O infrastructure and its attached I/O resources.

Can the I/O resources, both the physical resources and the virtualized resources, be dynamically managed to accommodate changing workload demands?

The ability to allow I/O resources to be dynamically managed and readjusted to meet changing workloads is fundamental to SOA workloads. System z provides a portfolio of I/O resource provisioning and management technologies to accommodate this requirement. For example, all of the system's physical I/O resources can be dynamically reconfigured. Channel paths, I/O adapters and all of their attached I/O resources may be dynamically and non-disruptively added, modified or removed to meet changing workload demands. System z also provides for the automatic adjustment of I/O resource sharing by "clusters" of logical partitions. It has the ability to reprioritize the execution of I/O operations by software operating within the resource sharing

partitions and to move I/O resources, such as channel paths, from one partition to another automatically.

SUMMARY

A robust and efficient server virtualization technology is vital to providing the flexibility demanded by the emerging class of SOA applications. The extent to which resources can be virtualized depends, to a large degree, on how integrated they are. The typical distributed server is constructed from a wide variety of hardware and software sources. This limits its ability to provide an integrated virtualization solution. To compensate, these servers rely on virtualization within a cluster, using the process of deploying work to the machine best able to handle it. While this improves distributed deployments, it is not nearly as efficient as a fully virtualized machine that allows resources to be dynamically redirected to work that needs it most. This deep virtualization can only be provided by centralized scalable servers that combine the hardware, operating system and middleware into a single, seamless, virtualized solution.

Fully integrated virtualization technology will continue to focus on the creation of new virtualized network technologies, as well as on the dynamic redistribution of virtual machine resources across physical server platforms. These technologies will ultimately yield a totally virtualized network that will be more autonomously configured, managed and adjusted to meet the ever-increasing changes of the enterprises they serve.

Les Wyman joined IBM in 1965, retired in 1993 as a Senior Technical Staff Member and rejoined IBM in 1999. He's held numerous technical and technical leadership positions in programming, channel engineering and mainframe architecture during his career. Wyman has more than 20 years of experience in the conceptualization, design and architecture of mainframe virtualization capabilities. He's also achieved the ninth invention plateau and received numerous division and corporate technical achievement awards.

Chapter

◯ ◯ ⑩ ◯ ◯

MANAGING HETEROGENEOUS WORKLOADS

The variability of an SOA environment will test a system's capability to handle multiple heterogeneous workloads. But there are ways to consolidate the many elements of SOA composite applications into a single workload management domain to improve the efficient utilization of resources in the face of constantly variable consumption patterns.

BY ROBERT VAUPEL & CHRIS VIGNOLA

E fficient management of a machine's resources has always been an important element of managing cost. The harder a machine is driven, the less excess capacity is required to compensate for temporary deviations from steady-state resource consumption.

With the introduction of service-oriented architecture, "steady state" is a much more elusive metric to quantify. The very nature of SOA injects a lot more variability into the resource consumption equation. To a certain degree, and oddly enough, variability is the new steady state. This puts a lot more emphasis on the ability of an SOA deployment to utilize resources efficiently. Proper workload management becomes a critical factor in being able to perform to expectations.

APPROACHES TO WORKLOAD MANAGEMENT

There are two generally accepted approaches to workload management (WLM): entitlement-based; and goal-based. An entitlement-based system

 A CENTRALIZED DEPLOYMENT ALLOWS THE NATIVE WORKLOAD MANAGEMENT CAPABILITIES OF THE HOST PLATFORM TO PLAY A LARGER ROLE IN THE END-TO-END MANAGEMENT OF THE SOA APPLICATION.

assigns a specific share of CPU time to a workload. The work then consumes system resources based on the share of CPU time that's allocated. These shares are particularly enforced during periods of high system utilization where an assignment of CPU capacity (such as 30%) is reserved for consumption by a defined workload. This entitlement percentage is applied across any number of processors within a configuration. Entitlement-based workload management is policy enabled.

Unlike entitlement-based WLM, a goal-based WLM is abstract and, thereby, more flexible and applicable to an SOA environment. Typically, these goals are set in terms of operational performance within a set period similar to a service level agreement. Goal-based WLM defines a service in which it groups applications and transactions into a particular class. It then implements defined business goals derived from corporate objectives by prioritizing the importance of each service class.

This importance prioritization enables goal-based WLM to make decisions between service classes when the system reaches its maximum utilization. These goals provide a definition for end user response times and dictate how often an application can use system resources. For example, a goal for execution velocity will allow the end user to define how much work can be delayed while the application progresses through the system. The response time goal reflects a natural way that an end user interacts with a system. Someone standing at an ATM wants to get money from his checking account within several seconds.

To accomplish this, the service provider for the bank will require that each transaction be completed within five seconds. Since the entire transaction across all necessary infrastructures must take five seconds, then no more than half a second should be used to access the mainframe and the database repository. Therefore, a WLM goal can be derived directly from this objective.

Both centralized and distributed systems can implement a goal-based workload management system. There is, however, one big difference. The centralized system (specifically z/OS) can capture when a transaction begins and when it's complete and, thereby, measure how long it lasts. z/OS WLM (zWLM) monitors, controls and assures goal achievement. Since an SOA business service is, in essence, the consolidation of independent units of work, understanding when and how they're completed is central to effective management. It continuously collects state data of the system and checks every 10 seconds whether the goals are achieved or whether a change is necessary. If a change is required, zWLM projects how this change will impact all other service classes and other work on the system and adjusts the resource access. A change will only be applied if the projected value is in accordance with the importance of the service class. That's an important distinction between zWLM and workload management functions on all other platforms.

This unique function anticipates the impact of a component change, but will alter the service only if its service class is not negatively impacted. Measurement this granular requires both instrumentation and supporting middleware infrastructure and allows workload transactions to be managed at that level, not just at the process level. Only System z's z/OS provides such complete goal-based workload management that integrates the hardware, operating system and middleware into a single management domain.

SOA IMPACT

Within a service-oriented architecture, application components and processes used by SOA are actually either collections of independent work units or a type of transaction. WLM provides visibility into units of work currently running and already terminated. From this, a mapping of these entities to service processes and system threads can be conducted. This allows related entities or web services to be managed according to how a customer may classify them.

These processes and threads can reside on a single system or on different systems. When they are consolidated, that system's WLM capability (zWLM, for example) can be applied to the entire SOA application. When components are distributed among a set of different systems, the application of an enterprise or end-to-end workload manager (eWLM) is required. This eWLM collects information from all impacted systems. It then sends commands to each system to alter their behavior and, ultimately, the flow of the work. When a workload is distributed in this fashion, the WLM capabilities residing on the individual systems will be limited in influencing the flow of work across the middle-ware applications on other platforms.

THE CENTRALIZED SERVER ADVANTAGE

As noted above, a centralized deployment allows the native WLM capabilities of the host platform to play a larger role in the end-to-end management of the SOA application. In addition, a centralized server will have much less network latency. Since all components of the application are running on the same hardware and, potentially, the same operating system image, there's no need to initiate network calls to communicate between the components or incur delays while the thread of execution changes. The application also enjoys the benefits of co-location with its databases. In a distributed system, a process or service may have to travel to several servers and wait for processing.

It may also be subjected to multiple management philosophies, as well as the vagaries of crossing several network boundaries.

Finally, there is the performance issue. A distributed environment that's relatively under-utilized may experience good performance. As utilization rises, however, performance may decline. The direct cause of this performance degradation is often not obvious and, hence, difficult to address. In contrast, a centralized server keeps most activities under direct control. It monitors every instance and presents few boundaries that need crossing. Even a boundary cross from one middleware application to another is considered a local call not requiring cross-networking.

WLMs currently do not enable end-to-end cross system management in a distributed environment. It's one of the objectives of eWLM to make this happen. Even though distributed systems have local workload management functions, most of these servers run just one application because these local WLM functions were designed to execute all work within the server in the same manner; they are not capable of efficiently prioritizing competing workloads. On centralized servers, there are always multiple workloads running. This environment insists on the ability of the WLM to prioritize different types of work.

Both centralized and distributed systems can implement a goal-based ⊚ SOA SECRET workload management system. There is, however, one big difference. The centralized system (specifically z/OS) can capture when a transaction begins and when it's complete and, thereby, measure how long it lasts. z/OS WLM (zWLM) monitors, controls and assures goal achievement. Since an SOA business service is, in essence, the consolidation of independent units of work, understanding when and how they're completed is central to effective management.

When a workload is sent to a system, if there is less work to do than available system resources, then there is no problem. Every task receives as many resources as it needs and can run at full speed. When there are more workloads on the system than the system can support, there has to be a way to prioritize. The more information the system has about each workload, the better it can rank the need. This is particularly true if the system can enable the user to assert policy that provides structured insight into how the workloads differ, their relative importance to each other and existing performance goals. In other words: the expectations the user has of each workload's performance.

Hardware Advances Drive Need for eWLM

Centralized hardware platforms, such as System z, that enable the configuration of multiple logical computers that respond to demand from these different systems, are logical in nature and physically located on the same system, and are able to move CPU and memory between them within established parameters. This allows the physical computing resources to float across logical partitions based on relative demand and usage.

Borrowing from this concept are emerging technologies, such as IBM's WebSphere, that can combine some of the disciplines necessary to better utilize unused capacity in a distributed computing model, and apply similar techniques to centralized systems when they're used in clusters. An example of this clustering is in the z/OS disciplines, where multiple systems are interconnected with shared memory. The software built to run on that environment knows how to distribute that shared memory device and how to communicate with each system to provide horizontal scale.

That type of scaling tends to be very specific within the overall software stack that supports end user solutions. What tends to be lacking in a distributed deployment, however, is an intelligent way to dole out incoming workloads across this infrastructure. Unlike Oracle, where much of its workload originates directly on the platform, with SOA, it's very common for the point of work origin to shift to a source that may have previously been only a niche player on the shared system. The more common an application, the more likely it is to reside on a distributed system. This has been, and continues to be, a growing trend. As an SOA application starts to span multiple platforms, a centralized infrastructure is no longer the only place where that solution may reside. Nevertheless, these distributed applications also need a central place to host many of its services.

While SOA applications can be deployed to multiple logical partitions on a single physical machine, it is equally valid to utilize multiple physical machines to eliminate single points of failure. This results in several physical boxes, all with some number of logical partitions. So, as the virtualization technology in the physical box facilitates the movement of physical computing resources to meet the needs of the logical partitions, workload management capabilities within the logical system must effectively manage those resources within the SOA environment. That is similar to the problem a distributed environment must address. The work is coming from outside the system to a cluster of physical machines that allocate the workloads.

Work Routing
A product like WebSphere Extended Deployment (WebSphere XD) can address the challenge of workload routing. It has routing technology

---

The more common an application, the more likely it is to reside on a » **SOA SECRET** **distributed system. This has been, and continues to be, a growing trend. As an SOA application starts to span multiple platforms, a centralized infrastructure is no longer the only place where that solution may reside. Nevertheless, these distributed applications also need a central place to host many of its services.**

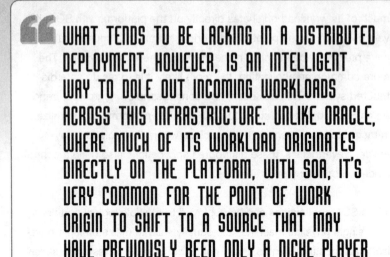

> WHAT TENDS TO BE LACKING IN A DISTRIBUTED DEPLOYMENT, HOWEVER, IS AN INTELLIGENT WAY TO DOLE OUT INCOMING WORKLOADS ACROSS THIS INFRASTRUCTURE. UNLIKE ORACLE, WHERE MUCH OF ITS WORKLOAD ORIGINATES DIRECTLY ON THE PLATFORM, WITH SOA, IT'S VERY COMMON FOR THE POINT OF WORK ORIGIN TO SHIFT TO A SOURCE THAT MAY HAVE PREVIOUSLY BEEN ONLY A NICHE PLAYER ON THE SHARED SYSTEM.

which resides in front of the physical systems and divides the work between them in an intelligent manner. WebSphere XD is more than just a round-robin smart switch. It interfaces directly with individual systems' workload management facilities and establishes a cooperative relationship between the centralized platform and the routing agent by making the decision of where to send inbound workloads. It's able to share information about the state of all the logical partitions within the systems and, thereby, establish the relative utilization of both logical and physical computing systems. This information is then used by the WebSphere XD router to distribute the incoming workload based on the same criteria employed by the native WLM.

An important, yet subtle, contrast demonstrates how a centralized system can more effectively manage heterogeneous workloads than a distributed system. A case could be made with regard to a centralized system's management characteristics. With fewer systems, it can maximize unused capacity, whereas distributed environments typically deploy many more systems, resulting in greater maintenance and management demands. That also means more network connection points to manage and more unused headroom.

While a product like WebSphere XD can help a distributed environment to improve its exploitation of unused capacity, it can only do so within certain limitations. A major inhibiting factor is that it can only manage a system's workload that's under its direct control. If there is another workload manager accepting work on the platform, it will undermine WebSphere XD's ability to manage the resources. In effect, no resource can be ruled by more than one master. As long as the workload is managed by a single workload manager, it works fine. Otherwise, there is confusion as to which one has control over the resources and can allocate workloads accordingly. So that's an inherent problem in a distributed environment. Factors like this discourage heterogeneous workloads from being hosted on distributed platforms.

In a centralized environment, the workload management mechanisms are not isolated from each other, but work together to coordinate a platform's resources and account for current workloads' relative importance and goal performance, as well as unused capacity. Therefore, the routing agent can make an informed decision on where to direct new work requests.

A distributed environment that's relatively under-utilized may » **SOA SECRET** experience good performance. As utilization rises, however, performance may decline. The direct cause of this performance degradation is often not obvious and, hence, difficult to address. In contrast, a centralized server keeps most activities under direct control. It monitors every instance and presents few boundaries that need crossing. Even a boundary cross from one middleware application to another is considered a local call not requiring cross-networking.

There is a wide spectrum of capabilities with regard to workload routing technologies. They range in intelligence from primitive round-robin mechanisms to systems like WebSphere XD that are able to profile work passing through it, then route it based on criteria set by the z/OS workload manager. As long as there is available capacity, the decision of where to send work is easy, with little need for management. However, it gets complicated and requires more sophisticated systems when there's not enough resources for the sum total of the workload that needs processing.

The service's importance level assigned by zWLM is critical because when resource demand exceeds its availability, it is allocated according to importance level. In other words, the more important work receives a bigger share of the resources. An outboard routing agent, such as the WebSphere XD routing agent, classifies and profiles work and provides an estimate of needed resources to zWLM. The zWLM can then feed back to the routing agent that it does not have any available unused capacity, but it does have capacity that's currently being used by less important work. This less important work can then be stopped and its resources reassigned to work with the higher priority.

Even in a constrained execution scenario where the sum total of work exceeds available resources, these systems can intelligently manage work from initial contact through the assignment of physical resources, all by applying the same policy. The combination of this layered workload strategy provides an effective management of mixed workloads for centralized resources.

Finally, the top-level tier of the workload manager pyramid is the intelligent routing methodology. This provides an important foundational element for effectively enabling the hosting of services in an SOA environment. It makes a centralized system a strong and effective deployment solution.

THE INTEGRATED BUSINESS GRID

An integrated business grid is an array of available, acute facilities that are applied to various computing tasks. The grid is not assumed homogeneous to the type of computing resources that are deployed. It reflects business requirements that are deployed on multiple different platforms and/or operating systems and hardware assembled to address various business needs. Hence, homogeneity is a natural consequence of determining which of the many available systems can process a particular workload type. It's actually relative to the workload itself.

The purpose of an integrated grid is not to throw everything out and start over. At its core, the promise of a grid environment is to exploit and leverage many of the systems in place today and, by extension, provide a management discipline across them that can effectively leverage a grid-like environment. This will enable an intelligent agent to assess a workload and decide, based on a variety of information, its type and then appropriately assign to a system within the grid to run. With more available knowledge, the workload manager can perform a better job in deciding which of the available machines is optimal to run this workload. This suggests that as work enters into the grid, the WLM will need to understand its requirements completely.

The integrated grid is analogous to pools of homogeneity within a larger ◆ SOA SECRET ocean of heterogeneity. To manage the grid effectively, the agents that distribute its workload need that type of information. The technology to accomplish this is still emerging. Grid-exploiting technologies are showing up in several products. For example, a grid scheduler is able to take inbound work and conduct the execution requirement.

These requirements include the applications and programs it needs to run, as well as necessary data and required access to other types of systems, like network connectivity. The routing agent then starts to look a little bit more like a scheduler. Work comes in and is classified. The WLM looks over the array of available computing resources to identify available capacity. However, since the machines in the grid are heterogeneous, it's not enough to identify a machine with excess capacity. The available systems in the grid are bound not only by the function that identifies its availability, but first and foremost by the fundamental distinction of whether the incoming work can be satisfied by that available system. The grid, for that particular workload, then becomes a subset of systems which can conduct the type of work requested based on its execution requirements. These execution requirements and performance requirements combine in the context of the grid to segment which systems can support the incoming work. Out of those systems, the best candidate is selected based on capacity, resources and availability.

The integrated grid is analogous to pools of homogeneity within a larger ocean of heterogeneity. To manage the grid effectively, the agents that distribute its workload need that type of information. The technology to accomplish this is still emerging. Grid-exploiting technologies are showing up in several products. For example, a grid scheduler is able to take inbound work and conduct the execution requirement. The classification can already be handled with WLM, so workload execution can be addressed by the ability to choose from among multiple systems to determine which one actually has the required program installed for the execution.

The WebSphere XD product version currently under development is being extended to allow execution requirements for workload types and to take into account other requirements. This version will also facilitate the management of the grid and offer the ability to install programs dynamically on target end points. The result will be more on dynamic demand capabilities available for exploiting and leveraging compute resources.

SUMMARY

Goal-based workload management is one of the keys to effective utilization of resources in an SOA environment. Centralization of heterogeneous workloads under a single native workload manager, such as that provided by z/OS, provides a number of advantages over infrastructures that rely on distributed workload management techniques. Even in situations where full consolidation of an end-to-end SOA composite application is not possible, adopting techniques that leverage the native WLM capability as much as possible will provide the most satisfactory results.

WebSphere XD improves overall workload management and resource optimization for OLTP in a System z environment. It accomplishes this by pushing the classification-resource, allocation-resource and consumption-goal-attainment control and feedback loop out to the work routing tier. From here it's able to coordinate and be optimized across the entire System z deployment.

WebSphere XD improves grid job scheduling by applying the WLM capabilities previously enjoyed only by OLTP workload to grid jobs. WebSphere XD thus can facilitate System z's ability to manage and balance this mixed workload. WebSphere XD will continue to deliver leading edge grid support, including support for increased resource heterogeneity and resource-based job scheduling for grid jobs.

Robert Vaupel worked for 20 years at IBM Germany after acquiring a master's degree in computer science at Germany's University in Karlsruhe. Since his entrance in IBM he's focused on performance and workload management of IBM's mainframe operating system z/OS. Today he is an IBM senior technical staff member and responsible for the development of the Workload Manager component of z/OS.

Chris Vignola is a Senior Technical Staff member who's worked at IBM for the past 22 years. His current work focuses on delivering business grid computing solutions, combining the best of grid scheduling, transaction, workload and resource management. His past experience includes work on systems management, J2EE, workload management, batch processing and peer and hierarchical distributed computing across web and mainframe environments.

Chapter

⎕ ⎕ ⑪ ⎕ ⎕

SECURING THE ENTERPRISE

No doubt securing the enterprise is an ever-growing concern.
Companies seeking a protected environment for SOA workloads must
understand it's not just applications that must be safeguarded.
This may mean a major shift in evaluating security needs.

BY GARY PUCHKOFF & MIKE KEARNEY

Many organizations are using best practices developed during the days of client-server computing to evaluate their needs for service-oriented architecture. However, the characteristics of SOA workloads can differ from those of client-server applications, sometimes substantially. Security is one of those areas where SOA differs from client-server, calling for an adjustment in the way that security needs are evaluated. This chapter reviews the basics of traditional client-server security and then discusses some unique requirements introduced by SOA. It also introduces the technology to meet these requirements and its effect on the enterprise. SOA does more than build on the infrastructure used by the client-server environment. It requires security at the level of individual messages, which is a new concept to many organizations.

The basic aspects of security for a traditional client-server environment, and everything that held true there, continue to be valid in an SOA environment. But often, a client-server environment is typified by focusing on a

local area network where a company has some control over the network and the clients. With SOA, the environment can be much more open. After all, SOA is about connecting different business entities, corporations or clients to application systems. This, though, brings with it a whole new set of vulnerabilities and associated technologies to address these concerns.

SECURITY FUNDAMENTALS

There are three major aspects to securing an enterprise. One is identifying users through, typically, authentication. Second is authorization, or allowing those who have been authenticated to access a resource and then track what they use. Third is implementing multiple layers of security so if one component is compromised, another continues to thwart an intruder.

Identification and Authentication

First to be done is identify people who can access your systems by giving them usernames and then recording those names in some type of identity store. That store for the WebSphere Application Server can be an LDAP repository, a custom user registry or, in the case of WebSphere for z/OS, a System Authorization Facility (SAF) product like Resource Access Control Facility (RACF). In a distributed environment, each application is typically secured independently from other applications. In some cases, this means a highly fragmented set of authentication and authorization systems, databases and administration systems. This can create difficulties in maintaining the security of the overall system. In a mainframe environment, the security is more likely centralized and administration more consistent. As a result, it's less likely to be subject to correlation errors.

For example, in large enterprises the administration team that manages RACF is usually quite experienced and the security policies robust. The identity store contains the user's principle name as well as some other information to authenticate, such as a password. The

WebSphere Application Server provides an abstraction, called a registry, which supports a number of different types of registries, including Microsoft's Active Security and Active Directory. This provides an LDAP wrapper in an Active Directory to port many different kinds of LDAP servers. This is not an either/or decision between RACF and LDAP; the LDAP server for z/OS supports the use of the RACF database as the repository for passwords stored in LDAP. This means that users authenticating to a WebSphere application will use the same password to access their CICS, IMS or TSO account, and when they change their password in one place, it will be reflected in both places. This password consistency is important to maintaining overall security when existing business systems based on traditional transaction managers are incorporated into SOA processes.

This registry serves to identify users and supports an authentication mechanism. Attempting to access a resource that's protected on a WebSphere Application Server, for instance, will result in a challenge for authentication. In some cases, it checks usernames and passwords. But some organizations, such as banks, have more stringent security requirements that require additional factors to access core banking applications, typically digital certificates. Public key infrastructure (PKI) utilizes a certificate authority.

SOA SECRET

In a distributed environment, each application is typically secured independently from other applications. In some cases, this means a highly fragmented set of authentication and authorization systems, databases and administration systems. This can create difficulties in maintaining the security of the overall system. In a mainframe environment, the security is more likely centralized and administration more consistent. As a result, it's less likely to be subject to correlation errors.

A bank could utilize the z/OS Cryptographic Services PKI Services (a standard component of the z/OS operating system) or an outside certificate authority to issue and maintain client certificates. Each new ebanking customer would be sent one of these certificates, perhaps in the form of a smart card or an encrypted file to put into a browser. The WebSphere Application Server would then support authenticating that certificate and mapping it to an identity of the principle that's in the registry. When used as the user registry for WebSphere, RACF supports the mapping of the client's digital certificate to his RACF identity so that authentication can take place securely, without the need for a client password.

Some customers have two-factor authentication requiring both a certificate and a password, depending on the security needs of the application. Once authentication is complete, access to the requested resource is checked.

Authorization
Authorization is the act of controlling access to resources. There are several different types of authorization. The first is table-based, where a table is maintained in the WebSphere application that maps the principle and resource to one another. A resource is looked up and it's determined whether the principle is authenticated to that resource. This is not a very scalable solution, as the security information resides in the application, rather than in an external security manager.

A second type of authorization utilizes an external security manager, like Tivoli Access Manager. This product manages authorization data against a central repository of policies and allows access according to the application of those policies.

A third type of authorization is a standard JACC provider for Java authorization. Like the custom registry, this is a general authorization type that enables users to write any kind of authentication they choose. The JACC provider creates an interface that will conduct any kind of authorization.

Typically, what is authorized to WebSphere is authorized against roles. So servlets and Enterprise Java Beans (EJB) both have a place to configure what roles are required to successfully execute a particular servlet or a particular method on an EJB. In this manner, a user would be associated with a role and then permitted access only when in that role. The most popular type of authorization mechanism used in large enterprises is an SAF external security manager product, like RACF. RACF uses profiles and an administration process familiar to the enterprise security administration staff to support the definition and administration of J2EE roles for access to WebSphere applications. Considering banking again, employees include both tellers and supervisors. A teller might be allowed to look at balances for any customer, but someone in a supervisor role might also be able to create and delete accounts. This is a standard type of security used in client/server applications.

Web services security is concerned with securing the messages flowing back and forth and standardizing identification information and the authenticators. It doesn't really address authorization. There is very little in the web services specification that addresses how to authorize a web service; it just identifies the manner in which the authorization tokens can flow. In the case of most synchronous messages, authenti-

SOA SECRET

WS-Security has been an OASIS standard specification for some time and addresses security at the message or request level, as well as the SOA package level. It ultimately allows an SOA message to be trusted by the web services provider since the message can be digitally signed or encrypted. Web services security needs to be implemented at the application or container level so it's available on the server where the web service is running.

> **FIRST TO BE DONE IS IDENTIFY PEOPLE WHO CAN ACCESS YOUR SYSTEMS BY GIVING THEM USERNAMES AND THEN RECORDING THOSE NAMES IN SOME TYPE OF IDENTITY STORE.**

cation data can be sent back and forth. However, when considering asynchronous messages, like those produced by a product such as WebSphere MQ, there is very little standardization in the way users are authenticated because the message formats don't introduce any security information. Standard JMS or MQ message formats do not have any standardized slots for passing an identity. Therefore, what web services brings to the table is a transport-agnostic method of passing that security information and a way to authenticate users between totally disparate systems.

Auditing

Auditing is the discipline of tracking what resources have been accessed. Security auditing tracks who has accessed specific resources. It then records this information to determine who has manipulated a resource and whether that resource may have been misappropriated.

Within the context of SOA, all of these things apply, with the main difference being that SOA requests are going to come in through web services requests with a set of inter-operable security standards. Web Services—Interoperability (WS-I) is a web service specification that describes interoperability standards and, for security, defines token formats that allow different vendors of web services to interoperate and function securely. It defines security standards and creates a plan to send identity and authentication information to the server. The server will then unwrap that plan, validate and allow or refuse access to that resource.

Auditing is enhanced with the z/OS RACF operating system-based registry. This registry, from a security perspective, has a unique feature: it separates the duties of the security auditor and the security administrator. The security auditor is allowed to see or record all aspects of the security configuration including all of the actions the security administrator takes. The security administrator is allowed to change all aspects of the configuration of the security product with the exception of the auditing features. By separating these two responsibilities, the installation is more secure since it requires the collusion of two separated individuals to create an undetectable security breach. In this manner, the auditing performed by RACF and the other SAF products is more robust than those found on other platforms.

THE SPECIAL CASE FOR SOA

SOA security demands a different approach from web server security practices currently used in client-server applications. Presently, web server security is usually maintained between a client (most often a real person) and an application server. In this configuration, the client will conduct authentication of the server and the server will conduct both authentication and authorization of the client. Once the server authenticates the person acting as the client, it determines whether to allow a request to proceed.

Web services security is concerned with securing the messages flowing back and forth and standardizing identification information and the authenticators. It doesn't really address authorization. There is very little in the web services specification that addresses how to authorize a web service; it just identifies the manner in which the authorization tokens can flow.

» SOA SECRET

 THE IMPORTANT PART OF HARDWARE CRYPTOGRAPHY ISN'T JUST THE HARDWARE, BUT HOW THAT HARDWARE IS IMPLEMENTED.

SOA is more often server-to-server and requires a different approach to security. An SOA server will typically receive requests from other servers, which are themselves conducting a traditional client-to-server conversation with the actual client. The servers' identity will probably be known to the SOA server, but the clients' identity may not be. This requires both the traditional client-to-server security mechanisms and new mechanisms to enable security and establish trust between servers. Since SOA makes use of web services, the new mechanisms will rely on web services security.

The standard that applies to securing SOA messages is called Web Services (WS)-Security. WS-Security describes enhancements to SOAP messaging that provide quality of protection through message integrity, message confidentiality and single message authentication. These mechanisms can be used to accommodate a wide variety of security models and encryption technologies. WS-Security has been an OASIS standard specification for some time and addresses security at the message or request level, as well as the SOA package level. It ultimately allows an SOA message to be trusted by the web services provider since the message can be digitally signed or encrypted. Web services security needs to be implemented at the application or container level so it's available on the server where the web service is running. Digital signatures can then be used as a way to insure the authenticity of the message and encryption used to protect the contents of the SOA message.

WS-Security forms a basis for other security specifications that are being employed or will be employed by SOA. Web service security is still new, and some of the standards are still being defined or standardized.

WEB SERVICES SECURITY: AN EXAMPLE

Say an airline currently runs a web site where consumers can display flight information and reserve and pay for airline tickets. The airline then develops an SOA web service to provide the same capabilities for a new audience. This web service will be used by travel agents, tour operators and consumer service providers to arrange air transportation for their clients. These consumer service providers act as intermediaries between the airline and the ultimate client. Therefore, the client may have an account and a credit card on file with the intermediary, but not necessarily with the airline.

This situation exhibits several important aspects of SOA security. The relationship between the client and the intermediary utilizes traditional client-server security. The SSL or TLS protocol is employed to encrypt the conversation, protecting sensitive data, such as authentication or credit card information. The client authenticates with the intermediary using a user ID and password. Access control rules imposed by the intermediary will determine which operations the client can perform. As the purpose of the intermediary is to enable e-business, the intermediary requests or requires that the client provide credit card information so that it will be convenient and available during the purchasing process. This model of security is widely used in e-business today.

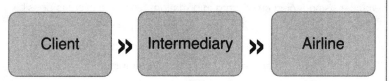

The relationship between the intermediary and the airline web service introduces a new set of security concerns. These concerns and the

technology required to address them depend on the nature of this relationship at a point in time. For example, when an intermediary is utilizing the airline web service to search for flights, the web service probably doesn't need to know the identity of the intermediary. Access to flight schedules is a public service. For performance reasons, it's best to use security services only when they're needed and to make them as granular as possible. Also, authentication and encryption is expensive. However, when the intermediary is attempting to reserve a seat on a flight on behalf of a client (i.e., money is going to change hands), the relationship between the intermediary and the airline web service changes.

For the intermediary, it's critical that the airline web service prove that it's authentic and not a hacker impersonating the airline and hoping to collect credit card information. It's also important that the client's credit card information be communicated to the airline web service in a secure manner. When the client completes a purchase, the transaction summary and receipt must be communicated securely and the integrity of information preserved. In other words, if the reservation confirmation information received by the intermediary is not exactly what was sent by the airline web service, the intermediary must be able to detect this, so it can ask for a retransmission or otherwise recover from the error.

It's important to the airline web service that the intermediary be a trusted business partner. This means the intermediary must be authenticated to the web service and prove that the intermediary is not a hacker using stolen credit card information. Since the client is possibly unknown to the web service, the web service must be able to trust that the intermediary has authenticated the client and taken reasonable precautions to ensure that the client's credit card information is authentic. It's important that the flight reservation request and the credit card information presented by the intermediary be communicated securely and the integrity of that information preserved. Like the intermediary, the web service must be able to detect if the information exchanged has been accidentally or intentionally modified. The authentication that will take place between a WebSphere server providing an SOA application, like the airline web service, and a trusted intermediary, like a travel agent, will most likely use SSL and digital certificates for both servers.

The airline example involving an intermediary illustrates how the security requirements of web services can range from minimal (a public web service) to maximal (authentication, message encryption and message integrity). Web services security is designed to provide the message level services security services need by SOA applications.

IMPLEMENTING SECURITY

SSL and cryptography are large consumers of machine cycles and drain capacity away from machine resources that would otherwise be available to do the actual business workload. In client-to-server networks, SSL can be offloaded from the application server by putting a firewall or an SSL appliance in front of the application server to handle the SSL work. It's worth noting that these SSL appliances, as standalone devices, introduce additional management (problem determination, key management) and environmental (space, heat) concerns. When this type of topology is used, the application server gets a request from the client that has already

> **» SOA SECRET**
>
> SSL appliances, as standalone devices, introduce additional management (problem determination, key management) and environmental (space, heat) concerns. When this type of topology is used, the application server gets a request from the client that has already been unencrypted so the application server doesn't have to devote any cycles to that task.

 AFTER ALL, SOA IS ABOUT CONNECTING DIFFERENT BUSINESS ENTITIES, CORPORATIONS OR CLIENTS TO APPLICATION SYSTEMS.

been unencrypted so the application server doesn't have to devote any cycles to that task.

But with SOA, signatures and encryption occur at the message level and have to be available at the application level and not in some appliance. If authentication and message integrity are not done at the application-server level, it would be buffered in the application across multiple platforms. Therefore, having high quality, high performance, cryptographic hardware available on the platform where the web service is run, and where these web service security operations take place, is a big advantage to implementing SOA.

The important part of hardware cryptography isn't just the hardware, but how that hardware is implemented. Most systems have hardware-based accelerated cryptographic services that are accomplished through an attached card. IBM System z supports attached card processing, but it also has the actual hardware operational codes that do hashes, encryption and decryption built directly into each CPU so that these critical security functions are processed with little overhead, and at chip speeds.

A company has little control over the architectures used by its business partners, but it can control where its own SOA applications are run. SOA applications will most likely be composite applications that incorporate existing core business systems which, in many cases, are hosted on a mainframe. From a security standpoint, just as with web applications, SOA applications will benefit from placement as close as possible to the existing business applications and data. Running the WebSphere Application Server in the same LPAR as CICS, IMS or DB2 allows the use of Type 2 connectors, which provide a higher degree of security granularity when passing authentication information between WebSphere and the business application. Running WebSphere in the same LPAR (or at least the same Parallel Sysplex) allows for the use of a common RACF database with improved security management and auditing capability for both the business applications and the SOA server.

A company that's fortunate enough to be able to host both the intermediary and the SOA applications (for example, its SOA applications are used only within its own intranet) will find the same to be true.

SUMMARY

SOA adds to the security challenges faced by the enterprise today. Security best practices developed in the days of client-server computing do not always hold true in the SOA world, which is predominantly server-to-server. With SOA, organizational security policies will have to focus on security at the message level. Standards such as WS-Security address these challenges. However, they come with the overhead and management costs associated with an increased use of cryptographic operations. As SOA implementations expand, the value of the security offered by the proximity and consolidation of data and components on a centralized server will become more apparent.

Gary Puchkoff is the Chief Architect for WebSphere on the z/OS platform and was one of the key IBM architects involved in the creation of the zAAP processor for off-loading Java processing on z. He has over 20 years experience in IBM, and has spent his career focused on the z platform, working on variety of software components. He is a frequent presenter at customer conferences and events, and has worked closely with a number of customers on their successfully deployments of WAS z/OS applications.

Mike Kearney is a System z security specialist with IBM's Washington Systems Center in Gaithersburg, Md. Mike joined IBM in 1978 and became a security specialist in 1990, earning his CISSP in 1997. He enjoys helping customers understand and configure security in WebSphere for z/OS.

Chapter

◻ ◻ ⑫ ◻ ◻

GOVERNANCE: MAINTAINING CONTROL

Some IT functions are best implemented in a distributed model.
But when it comes to SOA governance, maintaining better and tighter control
over critical aspects may require a quite different approach.

BY MIKE BENSON & DANIEL KABERON

Centralization is often presented as a panacea to simplify and facilitate adherence to a range of standards. However, it's also important to open up environments to a world of emerging services from every corner of what journalist Thomas Friedman has famously recognized as "the flattening world."[1] Gaining centralized control, while also enabling exploitation of the widest range of service-oriented architecture opportunities, must be the ambitious goal.

Maintaining control of a large enterprise can be a daunting task. All companies attempt to do this and many fail, thwarted by the shear complexity of the task. However, for an SOA to be successful, it must be governed well and, hence, kept under control. This chapter will address governance issues in a large scale enterprise from an SOA perspective and how centralization can help simplify the governance process and improve its effectiveness.

 AS THE NUMBER AND DISTRIBUTION OF INDEPENDENTLY DEVELOPED SERVICES INCREASES IN AN SOA, THE NEED TO CONTROL ACCESS TO THOSE SERVICES BECOMES EVEN MORE COMPLICATED. 🙶🙷

THE NEED FOR I.T. GOVERNANCE

Some companies fall into severe trouble by not having a system that's both accountable and auditable, leading to poor or ineffective system governance that impacts the bottom line. The results can be catastrophic, even resulting in bankruptcy.

In *IT Governance: How Top Performers Manage IT Decision Rights for Superior Results,* authors Peter Weill and Jeanne Ross describe IT governance as "a decision and accountability framework to encourage a desirable behavior." While this seems to be more process- than IT-oriented, the decisions that are made directly impact IT infrastructure. For instance, if a company has a decision-making process that pushes the selection of IT standards down to individual department levels, the resulting IT infrastructure will very likely look like the proverbial spaghetti chart. Corporate-wide integration becomes difficult, if not impossible, as each department chooses its own "standards" to follow. This environment is also a problem to manage since there is no simple way to view the entire IT process from end-to-end with a common set of tools. The infrastructure will most likely be less secure and less reliable. For many companies, this type of infrastructure is a sad reality.

However, some have recognized this problem and developed organizational entities to address it. An example of one or these organizational entities is the Enterprise Architecture Group (EAG). As with most over-

sight boards, if an EAG is implemented well, it can be the driving force behind a company-wide standardization that simplifies IT infrastructure and yields the necessary flexibility and agility. In a 2006 study conducted by the InfoWorld Media Group, fully 83% of companies responded that they have an EAG. However, just having an EAG does not guarantee success. An EAG can become a figurehead organization with little or no influence on actual IT implementations, or viewed as an "ivory tower" that makes decisions but never has to feel the pain of their implementation. Or, it can simply be ignored, which is often the case in companies where the variance process is simple and easy.

I.T. GOVERNANCE IN A SERVICE-ORIENTED ARCHITECTURE

SOA is not a new concept but rather a new way of implementing an old concept. It has always been known that application encapsulation and reuse were important processes that enabled flexible and efficient development of IT systems. In the 1980s, there were initial efforts to create reusable artifacts to reduce implementation time and, thus, reduce project cost. In addition, once the artifacts were adequately tested, their reuse improved overall reliability. Prior to that concerted effort, reuse methodology was simply one of finding existing pieces of code that did a similar thing, copying and modifying them.

A more systematic approach to software reuse can help reduce development time and effort, while improving overall quality. In addition, industry trends, such as object-oriented programming, have shown that encapsulation and reuse are not an isolated concept for a few

> **» SOA SECRET**
>
> A more systematic approach to software reuse can help reduce development time and effort, while improving overall quality. In addition, industry trends, such as object-oriented programming, have shown that encapsulation and reuse are not an isolated concept for a few esoteric programmers.

> **SOME COMPANIES FALL INTO SEVERE TROUBLE BY NOT HAVING A SYSTEM THAT'S BOTH ACCOUNTABLE AND AUDITABLE, LEADING TO POOR OR INEFFECTIVE SYSTEM GOVERNANCE THAT IMPACTS THE BOTTOM LINE. THE RESULTS CAN BE CATASTROPHIC, EVEN RESULTING IN BANKRUPTCY.**

esoteric programmers. In fact, a 2006 survey by Larstan Business Reports indicates that almost 90% of companies reuse software some of the time and 50% a good deal of the time.

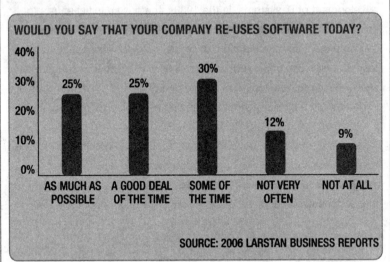

WOULD YOU SAY THAT YOUR COMPANY RE-USES SOFTWARE TODAY?

AS MUCH AS POSSIBLE	A GOOD DEAL OF THE TIME	SOME OF THE TIME	NOT VERY OFTEN	NOT AT ALL
25%	25%	30%	12%	9%

SOURCE: 2006 LARSTAN BUSINESS REPORTS

SOA has built upon the concepts of reuse and object-oriented programming by adding a business view and by strengthening implementation standards. Analysts, who understand the business processes of the company, can assemble the necessary services to create new business processes. The emergence of stronger and widely accepted standards, such as web services, has expanded the reuse opportunities for many business services.

With SOA, business services are created and then assembled into business processes, making effective IT governance even more critical. Defining new services, uncovering useful existing services and ensuring that they are reused properly are not trivial tasks. Also, ensuring adequate security and accurate auditing and correlating events within a complex system are not simple.

In the *InfoWorld* survey below, the No. 1 inhibitor of SOA adoption is the lack of governance in an enterprise. It outranked incomplete standards, lack of proper infrastructure or even the performance of the system.

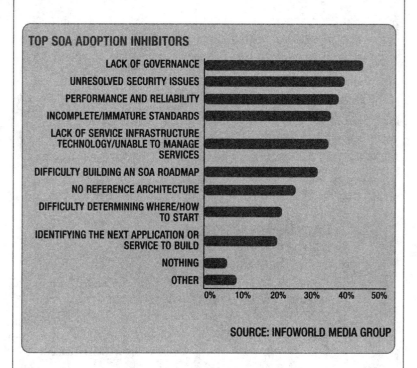

TOP SOA ADOPTION INHIBITORS

- LACK OF GOVERNANCE
- UNRESOLVED SECURITY ISSUES
- PERFORMANCE AND RELIABILITY
- INCOMPLETE/IMMATURE STANDARDS
- LACK OF SERVICE INFRASTRUCTURE TECHNOLOGY/UNABLE TO MANAGE SERVICES
- DIFFICULTY BUILDING AN SOA ROADMAP
- NO REFERENCE ARCHITECTURE
- DIFFICULTY DETERMINING WHERE/HOW TO START
- IDENTIFYING THE NEXT APPLICATION OR SERVICE TO BUILD
- NOTHING
- OTHER

0%   10%   20%   30%   40%   50%

SOURCE: INFOWORLD MEDIA GROUP

SOA IS NOT A NEW CONCEPT BUT RATHER A NEW WAY OF IMPLEMENTING AN OLD CONCEPT.

Companies moving toward an SOA are cognizant of the need to adopt effective governance models. Adoption has been progressing. Some 62% of companies in the *InfoWorld* survey said they currently have a software governance program in place. Of the remaining 38%, almost a third said that they will implement a program within the next 12 months. Twenty-three percent indicated no plans whatsoever. This is a disturbing statistic since it implies that a significant minority of companies do not yet recognize the importance of IT governance.

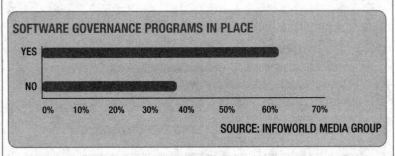

SOFTWARE GOVERNANCE PROGRAMS IN PLACE

SOURCE: INFOWORLD MEDIA GROUP

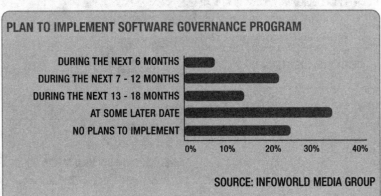

PLAN TO IMPLEMENT SOFTWARE GOVERNANCE PROGRAM

SOURCE: INFOWORLD MEDIA GROUP

IT GOVERNANCE IMPLEMENTATION STYLES

Much like IT systems, SOA governance can be implemented in either a centralized or decentralized control structure. A centralized governance style is similar to the EAG described earlier. A distributed style of governance is best employed when a company has vastly different lines of business that share few IT assets. Each unique line of business can then have its own version of an EAG that operates independently from all others. In this environment, a corporate group may also provide guidance, but the real control is done locally at each line of business. As companies migrate toward more cross-selling within their own organizations, a distributed style will become less effective because systems will need enterprise-wide integration.

Take a manufacturer that produces automobile engines, for example, where the engine is composed of many different component parts that are each individually assembled. In a centralized form of governance, the decision to use U.S. or metric-sized bolts is made once and implemented across all of the component manufacturing organizations. In a distributed style of governance, each component organization would choose whether to use U.S. or metric bolts. This decision would likely vary across organizations. While each component can then be manufactured successfully, there can be no sharing of bolts across the enterprise because there is no central decision-making body that enforces a common set of standards.

An IT example might be a specific service definition. If the control of service definitions is done through a centralized SOA governing board, there is a very good chance that the service will get maximum reuse and be very reliable. If the control of service definitions is done at individual organizational units, the degree of reuse will likely be less, and cross-organizational reuse unreliable and unlikely.

GOVERNANCE OF CENTRALIZED SYSTEMS

Some aspects of governance are much more readily implemented in a centralized system. The chart below lists some of those aspects. The boldfaced entries are discussed in more detail in this section.

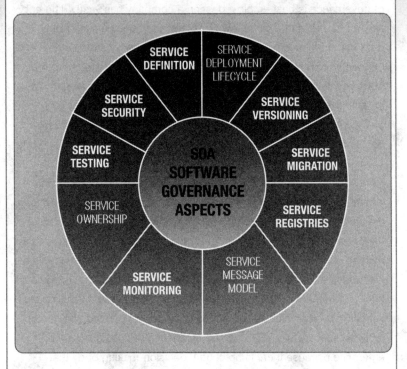

Service Definition

Unless an enterprise is starting from a green field with no existing IT systems or infrastructure in place, there will most likely be existing application functions that have already been deployed across the enterprise. Discovering those functions and determining whether they should be made into a common service can be a daunting task. This task is made more complicated when applications have been deployed across several different environments that use different implementation technologies and are owned by different organizations. Many companies have distributed their applications across Windows,

several UNIX versions, mainframe and other platforms. These applications have been written in many different languages, both procedural and object-oriented, and often their interfaces are proprietary.

Centralization is no silver bullet here. Even when centralized, an enterprise might still have numerous proprietary applications written in different styles and languages. However, centralized IT infrastructure can make it considerably easier to locate and assess existing assets to determine if applications could be converted to reusable services. Once they have been converted to a reusable service, putting them in a central service repository ensures that other potential users can find them quickly and exploit them efficiently.

Service Testing

Once a service has been defined and implemented, it must be tested. Reusable services in an SOA become critical single points of failure if they are not tested thoroughly. Whereas a single-use application may stop one function in the enterprise from working properly, an application that's being reused by several critical business functions can severely impact an entire company, should it become defective. For example, one company implements an enterprise service bus that several different application systems were using to gain access to common data. If that system has problems, due to any kind of failure, it will draw the quick attention of the CIO. When any type of outage occurs, the owners of that service would be on the "hot seat" to provide a quick solution to get the service back online.

> A major benefit of SOA is its reuse of a common set of services. Hence, there must exist a comprehensive listing of all services, including information on how to invoke them. A service registry provides that function.
>
> » **SOA SECRET**

THE NO. 1 INHIBITOR OF SOA ADOPTION IS THE LACK OF GOVERNANCE IN THEIR ENTERPRISE. IT OUTRANKED INCOMPLETE STANDARDS, LACK OF PROPER INFRASTRUCTURE OR EVEN THE PERFORMANCE OF THE SYSTEM.

Centralizing these types of mission critical services can help simplify the testing and ensure that it's complete, comprehensive and conducted at a lower cost. Deploying these same critical services across several different distributed platforms can elevate the cost of testing considerably.

Service Versioning
Taxes, death and change are the only certain things in this world. Services that are developed today will probably need to be changed or enhanced tomorrow. A business that does not adapt to change is probably doomed to failure. However, many users of an SOA service may not actually need any changes being made to it – the changes may have been made to support a new business process inapplicable to them.

One of the worse things that can happen when changing a widely used service is that the other existing users of the service no longer get the desired results. Services such as this are referred to as "brittle" because any change can break them. A versioning mechanism needs to be deployed to manage services successfully so that no adverse disruption occurs when a service is modified or enhanced. A strong centralized source code library management system can simplify service versioning by allowing versions that are currently being used to be easily tracked and by introducing newer versions in a controlled environment. Typically, in a centralized system, the testing and production environment are identical, so newer versions are thoroughly tested prior to their implementation.

Service Registries

Once services are created, they need to be made consumable. A major benefit of SOA is its reuse of a common set of services. Hence, there must exist a comprehensive listing of all services, including information on how to invoke them. A service registry provides that function. In addition, it can indicate specific service versions so that users understand its specific functionality. Service registries can also maintain access information for specific applications.

As with any information repository, the more it's distributed, the harder it is to keep synchronized. A centralized service repository is much easier to maintain and update. Far fewer service definitions will become out of date and migration to new versions can be done in a controlled manner. System needs for availability and scalability preclude an environment with only a single service repository. However, centralizing the management of a disparate group of repositories is simpler and more effective than attempting to manage them individually across the enterprise.

Service Monitoring

Successful deployment of all IT services requires adequate monitoring.

> **» SOA SECRET**
>
> Once a service has been defined and implemented, it must be tested.
> Reusable services in an SOA become critical single points of failure if they are not tested thoroughly. Whereas a single-use application may stop one function in the enterprise from working properly, an application that's being reused by several critical business functions can severely impact an entire company, should it become defective.

> UNLESS AN ENTERPRISE IS STARTING FROM A GREEN FIELD WITH NO EXISTING IT SYSTEMS OR INFRASTRUCTURE IN PLACE, THERE WILL MOST LIKELY BE EXISTING APPLICATION FUNCTIONS THAT HAVE ALREADY BEEN DEPLOYED ACROSS THE ENTERPRISE. DISCOVERING THOSE FUNCTIONS AND DETERMINING WHETHER THEY SHOULD BE MADE INTO A COMMON SERVICE CAN BE A DAUNTING TASK.

There are two main approaches. The first keeps technologies in silos; the second involves a centralized group whose expertise is systems management. Experience has demonstrated that when technology silos are responsible for monitoring, the task rarely receives high priority and critical holes often go unaddressed. A centrally focused systems management team that's cognizant of all of the organization's objectives and targets is often more successful in conducting this task. Governance of an SOA implementation must insure that the central systems management function is engaged. These monitors should simultaneously meet the technical needs of these distinct audiences and objectives.

» **Central Enterprise Operations:** This group needs a real-time view of performance as it relates to negotiated service level agreements. It also needs a clear view of problems within all infrastructures under its control.

» **Capacity Management:** This group requires hardened data that's summarized at a common interval length (typically 5, 10 or 15 minutes). This data is essential for developing and maintaining an understanding of the relationship between workload volumes and logical and physical resource utilization. This ensures that adequate capacity is implemented or made available to meet all business needs in the future and at the required service levels.

» **Resource Accounting:** SOA can be viewed as both the opportunity for existing business services to expand, as well as to create applications composed from several sources. With the breakdown of traditional hierarchies, where services and customers are strictly aligned, a fair scheme to assign costs is essential. SOA providers will not be eager to provide services if their consumers do not pay a fair share of costs. Similarly, SOA consumers will be disinclined to incorporate services if they do not perceive their costs to be fairly attributed to their business activities. Resource accounting data must measure and record *what* service is being consumed, *when* it was consumed, *who* consumed it (and at an appropriate level of granularity) and *how much* service was consumed.

Enterprise Performance Monitoring should always enable a meaningful answer to the common question: "How's it going?" Performance has only two dimensions: how much (the transaction rate) and how fast (the response time or the percent under threshold). The transaction rate tells us something about service productivity. Knowledgeable operations staff members that pay attention to their monitors are attuned to what comprises a typical performance. Major departures from expected performance need to be investigated. A significant drop in transaction rate is a very strong indicator of a problem, even if response time looks excellent. The transaction rate is often the best primary metric for evaluating performance results.

Repeatability and fairness must be sought. A good accounting metric ⊛ **SOA SECRET** **must vary according to the underlying resource consumption and collect similar results over a range of operating times and conditions. Note that precision per se is not necessarily important.**

 SERVICES THAT ARE DEVELOPED TODAY WILL PROBABLY NEED TO BE CHANGED OR ENHANCED TOMORROW. A BUSINESS THAT DOES NOT ADAPT TO CHANGE IS PROBABLY DOOMED TO FAILURE.

Generally, application monitors are either active or passive. Active monitoring employs the periodic execution of a script that performs a set of transactions deemed representative of user activity. Since the requested work is identical from one interval to the next, detection of anomalies in the service-delivery chain is trivial. The active monitor is especially valuable at recognizing problems during intervals when the transaction rates are near zero. Finding problems before the users become upset is essential to maintaining high availability.

There are several disadvantages to active monitors. First, the actual work requested by a system's users changes over time. As these changes occur, active monitors may stop hitting the most frequently used elements of the application. This can lead to a misleading view of performance. The active monitor also incurs overhead. Since the synthetic load is processed on the system providing service to the real users, the workload to accomplish monitoring competes with real work. If the work frequency is low, this is maybe insignificant, but at high work frequencies a company using active monitors may be working at cross purposes. Furthermore, scripting transactions can require secure user system identities, passwords and execution. Perhaps the greatest problem of the scripted workload is that it can easily break when the application it monitors is changed. Maintaining scripts to avoid false problem reports and maintain generally trustworthy reporting is a constant challenge.

Passive monitoring involves gathering data from normal work running on monitored systems. This identifies which transactions and specific user groups are more active at a point in time. It also presents real transaction loads and systems' responsiveness. Passive monitoring requires middleware or other tools that decode flows in the network. When work is encrypted, such as in SSL transactions, credentials must be shared with the monitors to gain a detailed view of the work and decode the workflows. Not all sites are conducive to sharing these credentials.

Best practices for performance monitoring include gathering data passively and reporting only the most informative measures. Thus, reporting the name of the user group or family of transactions, the transaction volume and those above the 90th percentile, as well as the median response time, may be adequate. This view should always be sorted by descending volume to make the heaviest hitters appear at the top.

SOA workload-supporting infrastructure can be monitored in many ways. SOA obviously puts more demands on a distributed network. It also makes it less likely to directly manage and monitor all the constituent components as more user groups access applications within that infrastructure. Monitors need to dynamically map the overall topology and decompose response time into its constituent delays. This is needed to enable effective problem determination and consis-

> **SOA SECRET**

Each unique line of business can have its own version of an EAG that operates independently from all others. In this environment, a corporate group may also provide guidance, but the real control is done locally at each line of business. As companies migrate toward more cross-selling within their own organizations, a distributed style will become less effective because systems will need enterprise-wide integration.

tent achievement of service objectives. Business Systems Management (BSM) is more important than ever in mapping infrastructure to the applications and business areas supported.

Capacity management efforts are primarily devoted to assuring that the services and organization hosts meet their objectives. The data from ongoing operations will need to be mined both to determine actual performance issues and to find customers (and how they are actually using the systems).

Resource Accounting is an activity that's mostly undeveloped among monitoring capabilities and general competencies. Its goal is to relate all costs associated with the provision of a service to metrics that are simultaneously understandable to the business sponsors and correlated to the actual underlying infrastructure costs. Accounting should not become a confusing and complex shopping list of raw service ingredients.

If efficiency is under the direct influence of the user and actually impacts delivery costs, it makes sense to separate costs. For example, it may be cheaper to use resources outside prime time hours. The time of day when work is accomplished must make sense to carefully consider different usage rates for prime and off-prime times. However, if the amount of memory work consumed is related to whether the data was previously cached, or when competing work was running, then charging for memory usage may not be optimal since users may not understand what they are being charged for. Additionally, that capacity is not directly under the users' control.

Charges should also be deducible from individual data records. That is, usage should not be determined by subtracting ascending fields from successive records with a master list. Fully defined records greatly facilitate both the data capture and archive/auditing functions.

Determining *who* consumes a resource is central to the accounting process. *Who* needs to be resolved to the level that assures that the correct entity is billed and any questions about the source of consumption sensibly answered. A service may be offered to answer the who, while in other cases, the division, location or fully formed charge code number may be necessary. Determining how to capture this data before the service is consumed and finding a sensible way to validate it can dramatically reduce the resources not billable and thereby improve the overall fairness of the cost allocation, which can actually reduce unit costs since all units will be billed accurately.

Level of consumption may or may not be difficult to account for. If all resource requests are approximately equal, simply counting the requests and charging them equally (with or without off-prime discounts) may be appropriate. However, when there is a wide spread of resource consumptions, then depending on the request, more detailed resource capture is appropriate. Repeatability and fairness must be sought. A good accounting metric must vary according to the underlying resource consumption and collect similar results over a range of operating times and conditions. Note that precision per se is not necessarily important.

SERVICE SECURITY

A major part of any IT system governance includes the security needed to prevent unauthorized access. There are many ways that IT systems can be compromised, and diligent prevention is an absolute

> » **SOA SECRET**
>
> SOA obviously puts more demands on a distributed network. It also makes it less likely to directly manage and monitor all the constituent components as more user groups access applications within that infrastructure. Monitors need to dynamically map the overall topology and decompose response time into its constituent delays.

necessity. Lately, there have been many compromises of data landing in newspaper and television headlines and causing significant loss of confidence in companies. Some companies have even lost revenue as a result.

The *InfoWorld* poll previously cited indicates that companies do place a high priority on the security of their systems. Even though it can be difficult to prevent unauthorized accesses, most companies are spending a lot of money to reduce the risks.

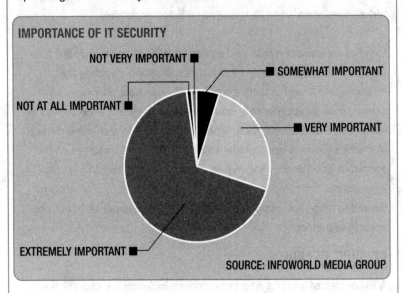

IMPORTANCE OF IT SECURITY

SOURCE: INFOWORLD MEDIA GROUP

Security in an SOA environment can be even more difficult since the services are typically independently developed and owned, and business process owners make use of them as needed to develop composite applications. Because the services are used in various applications, they need to pass security credentials to protect the data that flows between the service consumer and service provider to ensure that they are not vulnerable to being spoofed or intercepted.

As the number and distribution of independently developed services increases in an SOA, the need to control access to those services becomes even more complicated. A composite application may invoke individual services running on many different platforms with various security requirements. Centrally locating services can help ease the problem of security services since data is not passed as frequently over networks, and centralized security policies and procedures can be established and enforced. With fewer network hops, there are fewer chances of data being compromised.

SUMMARY

By centralizing the SOA governance model, companies can simplify their IT processes and procedures and ensure that they are within internal compliance goals and external regulatory mandates. Implementing a distributed IT governance model inherently results in less control. However, as previously mentioned, companies with vastly differing business units may need to distribute their governance aspects, but typically this is an exception, not the rule.

Mike Benson is a certified software IT architect in software sales working with companies in the northeast United States. He has been with IBM for more than 22 years, where he started in operating systems development for MVS in Poughkeepsie, N.Y. He has held a variety of positions over his career, including line management and software architecture and design. He currently holds two U.S. patents, has received several formal awards for his technical contributions, and has previously co-authored three IBM redbooks. He holds a master's degree in computer science from Marist College.

Daniel Kaberon graduated from the University of Chicago and became a research associate at The Thresholds, a psycho-social rehabilitation agency for former mental patients in Chicago. In 1989, he left mental

health and became a capacity management analyst at the First National Bank of Chicago where he applied his knowledge of statistics to computer performance and capacity. He joined Hewitt Associates in 1985 and currently manages nine technology managers leading a range of technical domains around large computer systems. He has earned one patent.

---

[1] The World is Flat: A Brief History of the Twenty-first Century, by Thomas Friedman, 2004.

Chapter 13

WHAT IT TAKES TO MAKE AN ENTERPRISE RESILIENT

The interdependence of systems involved in service-oriented architecture calls for a more durable enterprise. Here's guidance to reach that state.

BY BRIAN WOODS

In an SOA environment, system resiliency assumes a whole new level of importance. Organizations always have been subject to their systems' ability to avoid failure; but up to now, these failures were limited in scale (not depth) to one company and, maybe tangentially, to a small number of trusted suppliers. In this more localized scope of potential failure, it can be tempting to trade off quality in order to minimize cost. With service-oriented architecture, the resilience of each system takes broader, even global importance as one component can negatively impact core systems in several organizations. This chapter explores what it takes to make an enterprise resilient in the context of the requirements imposed by SOA.

RESPONSIBILITY AND RESILIENCY

Each company seeking the benefits of SOA must also assume the responsibility of being its brother's keeper and doing all it can to establish and maintain as high reliability as possible. Every company's infrastructure team will now have the responsibility to build something that's resilient. If enough

 EACH COMPANY SEEKING THE BENEFITS OF SOA MUST ALSO ASSUME THE RESPONSIBILITY OF BEING ITS BROTHER'S KEEPER AND DOING ALL IT CAN TO ESTABLISH AND MAINTAIN AS HIGH RELIABILITY AS POSSIBLE. "

redundancy is built in, then when individual systems go down, the total system can still react and service the complete business load. Whether an outage results in a small interruption to a particular service or a complete site failure, the need is to cover all of those events. Using System z clustering technology as an example, within a Parallel Sysplex system, clustered environment images and authentication services can be cloned. In addition, the number of ways that a database can be accessed can be cloned so that if a service or a system is unavailable, there are other ways to get in and conduct transactions.

Toronto, Canada-based TD Bank Financial Group is building an SOA service to authenticate user ID and password for its Internet banking customers. Some longtime employees of the bank would say that SOA has already been deployed in a number of places since there is a common architecture model for many existing banking transactions. These all were architected many years ago, well before the SOA buzzword became popular. While not exactly extreme implementations of SOA, these are common services built to accomplish a shared task, and that requires a high degree of resiliency. This approach has also standardized many common bank practices.

This common-services approach would certainly work on a distributed platform. However, most of the distributed platforms installed here are optimized for a single function. One or more servers are applied to one function, while another set of servers is earmarked for another. In contrast, the mainframe allows the integration of these applications so that they all run together in the same space. This reduces the complexity of hopping from machine to machine or from application to application on different platforms to collect the required information.

There are also some high-powered servers out there now with logical partitioning capability, much like the IBM mainframe, which can partition and run different copies of the operating system. However, with these systems, true sharing and running multiple workloads on the same box is achieved not with the hardware so much as with the operating system. The operating system enables several thousand different address spaces to run within the same box and provides virtualization.

IBM mainframe infrastructure virtualization provides the ability to do thousands of different things within one particular operating system image without, for the most part, worrying about one user interfering with another. Within the OS, everything is segregated into different address spaces and storage protection pools. Virtualization within a Windows or UNIX distributed environment is more like virtualizing different instances of the operating system on a physical box; each OS instance can still only handle one task at a time. The IBM mainframe virtualization allows it to do many things within the same copy of the operating system. That way with one OS, there is much less to maintain. Simplification of the infrastructure is central to high resilience. The fewer things there are, the fewer things there are to break, and the fewer things needed to integrate together.

> Virtualization within a Windows or UNIX distributed environment is more **» SOA SECRET** like virtualizing different instances of the operating system on a physical box; each OS instance can still only handle one task at a time. The IBM mainframe virtualizes to allow it to do many things within the same copy of the operating system.

ANOTHER WAY TO DRIVE UP AVAILABILITY IS BY BUILDING FOR REDUNDANCY AND ANTICIPATING ADDITIONAL CAPACITY NEEDED, BUT THIS REQUIRES THE ADDITION OF LARGE AMOUNTS OF CAPACITY THAT REMAIN UNUSED. 🙶🙶

The Limits of Simplification

Less is certainly better. However, it's still a challenge to make sure there is enough capacity available so that if something does break, the rest of the infrastructure can absorb the load. A single iteration is not the right answer. In TD Bank Financial Group's particular situation, the production configuration needs seven OS images to do the required work. There is capacity to pick up workloads should something fail and, if the machine does reach its physical processing limit, advanced workload management software takes over to ensure that the work with the highest business priority receives the resource required to meet business goals. Also, by using the System z environment and creating logical partitions (LPARs), capacity is available on demand, so if demand is greater than expected, capacity can be turned on temporarily (or permanently, if needed) to handle the load.

This is especially important in a failure situation. Extra engines can be turned on to pick up extra capacity during an extended outage. This is difficult to do in a UNIX environment because there is typically no excess capacity to turn to. Extra capacity can only be acquired by bringing on extra instances, which is not something that easily can be done on the fly or out of schedule. Another way to drive up availability is by building for redundancy and anticipating additional capacity needed, but this requires the addition of large amounts of capacity that remain unused.

THE IMPORTANCE OF TESTING

Another important practice: testing all components. A good, independent test environment is critical. Company policy needs to be set to test all changes being made, first to ensure that everyone understands what is being changed, and then to evaluate its impact. This obviously spans all environments. Any action for planned production must always be completed in a test environment first. Implementation procedures must be conducted to ensure not only that the system works, but also that it can be restarted after a failure. More risky changes should be subjected to several iterations to ensure that they are done correctly. A strong testing environment is important to the availability of an organization's systems.

Disaster Recovery: a Core Component of Resiliency

Business resilience encompasses not only the daily availability of an individual component or series of components, but also the ability to recover from a more catastrophic disaster, like the failure of an entire datacenter. A Parallel Sysplex, with a Globally Dispersed Parallel Sysplex (GDPS) implementation and synchronous mirroring, can capture all data. Using data mirroring through synchronization will ensure that before a business transaction completes, the information is

» **SOA SECRET**

Company policy needs to be set to test all changes being made, first to ensure that everyone understands what is being changed, and then to evaluate its impact. This obviously spans all environments. Any action for planned production must always be completed in a test environment first. Implementation procedures must be conducted to ensure not only that the system works, but also that it can be restarted after a failure. More risky changes should be subjected to several iterations to ensure that they are done correctly.

 AS SOA BECOMES MORE COMMON, AT LEAST WITHIN BIGGER COMPANIES, THE DEGREE OF SYSTEM CONSOLIDATION IS GOING TO BECOME AN IMPORTANT CRITERION IN COMPONENT SELECTION.

hardened at both remote locations. TD Bank Financial Group ensures rapid recovery with a synchronous copy between multiple sites, both of which are hardened. If the main production site goes off-line, the main production system can be restored within four to six hours with no data loss while operations continue to execute within business goals on the capacity that remains in the cluster.

Still, if all of a company's systems are centralized in one datacenter and it goes down, it means big trouble. Hence, a centralized system definitely needs to be able to recover from any outage, whether it's a single component or a complete datacenter failure. With the recent experience of regional failures and the power outages of a couple of years ago in the northeastern United States and Canada, it's also important not only to recover over a short distance, but also over thousands of miles or kilometers. Companies must consider if they need an additional datacenter that's geographically distant from its main production center.

By configuring infrastructure in this manner, compared to deploying a complex set of multiple pieces, system-wide reliability is kept high. At least one of TD Bank Financial Group's Parallel Sysplex systems has been running continuously for 9 1/2 years with at least one system active in that Parallel Sysplex at any point in time. During that period, every piece of equipment has been upgraded multiple times and many releases of operating system have been installed. Through all of this, the capability to push through transactions consistent with business goals was possible. This has been a huge advantage if you consider the alternative, which is to completely shut down your production services to implement changes.

Currently, many companies are considering consolidating their data-centers. Those with distributed servers are trying to consolidate a large number of datacenters to assume more control over them. They are also trying to consolidate servers by moving them back within an IT datacenter "glass house," so they can benefit from that center's hardening capabilities, such as dual power feeds and multiple network connections. Obviously this is the right thing to do — but it's far easier to execute when you are based on systems that were designed to run consolidated workloads in the first place.

SOURCES OF FAILURE

CPUs rarely fail. In general, the hardware is reliable. In most cases, it's the software that causes systems to go off-line. Any failure within the operating system, the transaction manager or the database manager will result in the system not being able to do any work. Although the hardware rarely fails, it's imprudent to think that it will never fail. Therefore, it's important to have redundancy for both software and hardware instances.

As work is spread across multiple platforms and operating systems, a point of failure becomes more likely. Assuming each individual plat-form is available 99.999% of the time, each link with another system of equal availability will reduce the total availability of cross-system

With SOA, an enterprise services hub matches the request for the service to **» SOA SECRET** the provider of that service. So, the services layer is important since it must ensure that these services are always available.

processes. Usually systems availability is the product of each component's availability. Therefore, two systems with 99.999% availability will have a systems availability of 99.998%. Each added system will reduce this percentage more. That's why, from the data standpoint, it's important to consider what is the minimum configuration needed to provide redundancy and resiliency.

Running an SOA infrastructure and applications on an architecture and in an environment that has a history of availability in the face of numerous system and operational changes is a major advantage.

CENTRALIZING REGISTRY SERVICES

SOA communicates to the services layer of the network stack. The application is the user of the services, and the infrastructure is the provider. With SOA, an enterprise services hub matches the request for the service to the provider of that service. So, the services layer is important since it must ensure that these services are always available.

There are advantages to having a central place to register services, but that central place must be highly available. In some ways, it comes back to infrastructure simplification. If services are spread across a thousand devices, then it's necessary to ensure that those services have registered their ability to function at a central point, so they will match the requester of the service with the appropriate provider. Thus, reducing the number of servers results in less points to manage. However, with this smaller number of points comes the need for each of them to always be on hand. In Parallel Sysplex, most systems are able to provide most services and the infrastructure is therefore simplified and services maintained so long as one of the OS images is still running.

Part of the services layer also needs to include data backup. Since data is critical, services must look after it. They need to provide data synchronization and replication to alternate sites. It's important to remember that if there's bad data caused by a bad application, synchronous data replications will replicate that bad information to the other locations. It doesn't provide protection from bad data, only from outages.

Therefore, services are needed to monitor data within the single site. A company will need to have backup, restoration and logging services to monitor who has been looking at, and accessing, data.

TO CENTRALIZE OR DECENTRALIZE?

Whether a company is best served with decentralized or centralized systems has been discussed for years now. Currently, many companies are consolidating equipment into a small number of datacenters. As SOA becomes more common, at least within bigger companies, the degree of system consolidation is going to become an important criterion in component selection. A component will either reside on highly resilient systems that can recover those components, or sit on a large number of replicated services, within one or more datacenters that enable failovers.

While both provide protection from system failure, the issue for a company becomes one of cost. When a company with a distributed system creates a configuration to manage failover, it does so by substantially increasing costs through redundant, extremely underutilized components. Distributed server environments often need to include

> **The most important part of recovery is the data. The work can be distributed across servers, but if the data cannot be distributed so that each work process is distinct, then distributing work has little value. It's necessary to insure data integrity, and the sure way to do that is by having all of these systems access the same backend that houses the production database.** » SOA SECRET

SOA IS ALL ABOUT REUSABILITY, BUT THERE IS MORE TO REUSABILITY THAN SOFTWARE OR METHODOLOGY. IT'S NOT JUST A TECHNOLOGY, BUT ALSO A WAY OF THINKING ABOUT AND CONDUCTING BUSINESS.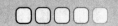

several additional servers for every production server being run. These will include, at a minimum, a disaster recovery server, a test server and a development server. Compare this to the Parallel Sysplex, which can run at a relatively high usage level and add capacity on demand, if needed, or utilize capacity backup processing power purchased at low cost. In essence, this configuration uses what was paid for and is only paying for what is used.

THE CENTRALIZED ADVANTAGE

The Parallel Sysplex shares resources. Therefore, a recovery site can have a production complex as well as development and testing capabilities. In the event of an outage at the main datacenter, the disaster recovery center can turn on some extra capacity and recreate all its capacity without losing a step. It does not need additional servers. A Parallel Sysplex system can be configured with excess capacity that's available at a low flat rate. This extra capacity can be turned on when needed to maintain or recover operations.

However, the most important part of recovery is the data. The work can be distributed across servers, but if the data cannot be distributed so that each work process is distinct, then distributing work has little value. It's necessary to insure data integrity, and the sure way to do that is by having all of these systems access the same backend that houses the production database. If the same data is being distributed over several locations and getting updated by various users and applications, then conflicts arise when updates are made at one site and not others. While there are some software replication applications, none provide the same snapshot possible with Parallel Sysplex and PPRC (Peer-to-Peer Remote Copy) synchronous data replication.

Grid computing and distributed grid computing will create pockets of computing power across the country. Therefore, if any one geographical area has an outage problem, there will be clear pockets of computing to fail over to. However, the problem with data remains. Where should the data reside? A financial institution with 10 million account holders is not going to allow its information to be replicated across 10, 20 or 40 different locations, for many reasons. Regulatory scrutiny is important, as are privacy, security and costs. Beyond these important constraints, other issues occur with reconciling several data updates that may be made to the same account information at different servers simultaneously. How will all of this be pulled together at the end of the day? Maintaining consistency is almost impossible when there are multiple copies of data.

SOA is all about reusability, but there is more to reusability than software or methodology. It's not just a technology, but also a way of thinking about and conducting business. Processes must be in place to identify existing components, including those that are reusable. This will establish a library of reusable components that developers can draw upon. By doing this, a company can become an entity trusted to

> **» SOA SECRET**
>
> SOA is all about reusability, but there is more to reusability than software or methodology. It's not just a technology, but also a way of thinking about and conducting business. Processes must be in place to identify existing components, including those that are reusable. This will establish a library of reusable components that developers can draw upon.

maintain these components and acknowledged for writing the best code and architecting a configuration that can be recovered from an outage. In the past, reusable components were intended to reduce development time. It failed because there was no buy-in from the development community and the cost to maintain these reusable components was high.

GETTING DOWN TO BUSINESS

SOA is designed to make things easier for developers. However, in essence, its purpose is to support a company's drive to be quicker to market since competitive advantage drives all companies. An enterprise that's too slow to the market eventually can't sell new product in an already saturated market. Nothing about SOA makes backend systems run faster. If anything, they may run slower due to the methodology used to access data or services.

With SOA, development costs are driven down, but unplanned performance overhead is added. What does that do to infrastructure? If overhead is spread across a large number of distributed systems, then a company may need more capacity. A shared environment, in contrast, may be able to handle these spikes in performance more transparently and at lower cost. What is unclear is how a full commitment to SOA will impact performance and drive capacity requirements. That's another area where a Parallel Sysplex can provide an advantage.

SOA will certainly not be faster. Companies need to understand this. Those SOA infrastructures running across a large number of servers may incur additional costs, as well as performance degradations. This may result in companies adding extra servers that negate all of the simplification benefits of SOA.

There are a number of activities done for resiliency, but at a performance cost. An example is implementing a GDPS and synchronous mirroring for disaster recovery. Internal users must be reminded that this activity to build resilience will, from a pure performance perspective, make things worse, not better. Every transaction is slowed because it must be written remotely, not just locally, before an answer is sent back. However, the benefit is that in a disaster, a good copy of the data is at hand and none of it is lost.

Brian Woods took his first information technology job as a co-op student in 1977. He recently achieved 25 years of service with TD Bank Financial Group. Until a few months ago, he spent his entire career working in mainframe infrastructure groups and ran the z/OS system programming and automation team for TD Bank for more than 14 years. He is a member of IBM's System z e-Business Leader's Council where he is the customer co-leader for the Business Resiliency workgroup and is also a member of IBM's GDPS Design Council. Brian has been an advocate of availability for many years explaining that the advantages of technology are lost if that technology can't be made to run in a highly available manner.

Chapter

◯◯⑭◯◯

MAINTAINING DATA AND TRANSACTIONAL INTEGRITY

Existing enterprise applications represent a rich stream of untapped
potential for reuse in SOA solutions. Here's how to do it without
compromising data integrity.

BY MARYELA WEIHRAUCH & STEVE WOOD

R egardless of an organization's service-oriented architecture vision,
data access and transactional integrity play a significant role in the
success or failure of an SOA initiative. Economics and competition put
tremendous pressure on IT departments to extract maximum value from
their organizations' existing applications. The quickest route to exploiting
this value is through reuse of existing transactional applications, by recreat-
ing them as renewable and reusable business services. In achieving this,
quality of service attributes, such as reliable, robust behavior, performance,
responsiveness and scalability, become an implicit expectation of the application users. Preservation of these characteristics is a critical success factor for new SOA solutions.

A successful SOA initiative requires infrastructure software specifically
designed to provide consistent performance and highly available data
across a computing environment. It must also support service behavior that
implements business logic deemed reliable in terms of transactions, data

integrity, performance, scalability, availability and security. The following chart illustrates the main reasons for unsuccessful SOA implementation and so demonstrates the requirements to be addressed for an environment optimized for SOA.

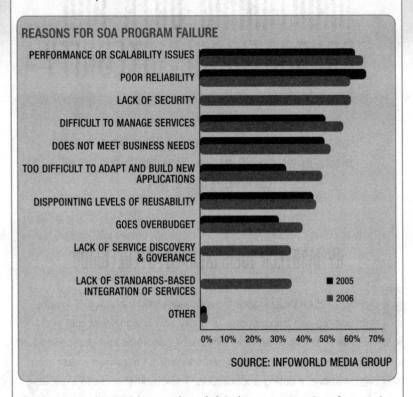

REASONS FOR SOA PROGRAM FAILURE

Business services relying on shared data in a concurrent environment require robust transactional characteristics. In an SOA where high concurrency is an important design consideration, the placement of transactional services in the architecture is important for achieving transactional robustness. Web service standards establish common transactional protocols between services. Distributed systems also implement environments that are able to coordinate transactions between platforms. However, where there is a need for highly concurrent, frequent updates of critical business data, centralizing the transactional services and shared data within a local environment can provide significant performance benefits. These tradeoffs are investigated in more detail later in this chapter.

THE IMPORTANCE OF TRANSACTIONS

What is a transaction, anyway? In a business application, a transaction is a single event or business item between two parties. A more formally stated definition is "an indivisible unit of work," comprised of several operations which may be performed to maintain data integrity.

A reliable business activity transaction between two parties is one that's guaranteed to be complete in whole, or not at all. This guarantee is achieved by ensuring that the applications and services that implement the transaction have "ACID" properties, described in more detail later.

As an example, consider a service that manages bank accounts. This service has three operations that could be invoked by another application within an SOA: add to an account; delete from an account; or move money between customer accounts. The most difficult of these services is to move money between customer accounts, because it must do whatever is necessary to ensure that all accounts are updated and that the transfer task is completed on each account. Serious problems would result if the server failed or the database contained errors after only some updates were complete. One customer could have his money withdrawn, without the other customer receiving any money (providing an unintended bonus for the bank). Or, both customers could receive money, resulting in an unintended loss for the bank. Also, since the component is designed to read the database to check whether there are sufficient funds and then update the database with the new

In an SOA where high concurrency is an important design consideration, the **» SOA SECRET** placement of transactional services in the architecture is important for achieving transactional robustness.

A SUCCESSFUL SOA INITIATIVE REQUIRES INFRASTRUCTURE SOFTWARE SPECIFICALLY DESIGNED TO PROVIDE CONSISTENT PERFORMANCE AND HIGHLY AVAILABLE DATA ACROSS A COMPUTING ENVIRONMENT.

balance, if two bank employees tried to move money from the same account at the same time, one of the updates could be lost.

THE ACID TRANSACTION

To prevent problems such as those previously illustrated, ACID transactions are created. ACID stands for atomicity, consistency, isolation and durability.

Atomicity. To be atomic, a transaction must execute completely, or not at all. This means that every file, database or queue operation within the transaction must execute without error. If any part of the operation fails, then the entire unit of work is terminated, which means that changes to the data are undone. There is no trace of the attempt to execute the transaction; however, a requirement may exist to log the start of a transaction for audit purposes. If all the operations execute successfully, the transaction can then be committed and changes to the data made permanent.

Consistency. Data must be consistent throughout the system. This means that the transaction, taken as a whole, does not violate any of the integrity constraints associated with the state of the resources. Obviously, the program itself is the arbiter of consistency in a business sense. In the above example, moving money should not alter the total amount of money in the accounts.

Isolation. Transactions should not affect each other's behavior. Isolation means that even though transactions execute concurrently, they appear to be serialized. In other words, to each transaction there's another that must execute before it, or after it, not simultaneously. SOA solutions are designed to address requirements for multi-user systems where different users access a shared database by utilizing transactional services via different means of interaction, such as portals or dedicated devices. In such a highly concurrent environment, isolation is a critical characteristic. When some, but not all, of the updates needed for consistency have been completed, the database is inconsistent. When all the updates have been completed but the transaction has not yet committed, the transaction could back out. In either of these cases, allowing other transactions to see or update records could result in errors in the database. Isolation means that other transactions can be prevented from seeing or updating the same records. In other words, the data that a transaction accesses cannot affect, or be affected by, any other part of the system until the transaction is completed. If moving money was not isolated, an inconsistent view of the database would be possible, or worse, concurrent updates could corrupt the database. Complete isolation is logically equivalent to forcing serialization of all transactions against the database, only allowing concurrent transactions to occur that do not affect each other in any way at all.

Implementing ACID properties by unique application code in every business service would be difficult. It would totally obscure the business logic, making the implementation difficult to maintain and audit. The problem is that some aspects of the implementation are not business issues, but technical ones. The technology should address them in order to ensure the implementation is as easy as possible to build.

SOA SECRET

Durability. Successful state changes must persist in the system. This means that after a transaction completes successfully, or commits, its changed state survives failures. This normally requires that all the data changes made during the unit of work must be written to some type of physical storage when the transaction is successfully completed.

Implementing ACID properties by unique application code in every business service would be difficult. It would totally obscure the business logic, making the implementation difficult to maintain and audit. The problem is that some aspects of the implementation are not business issues, but technical ones. The technology should address them in order to ensure the implementation is as easy as possible to build. This will allow the implementer of the business logic to focus on business issues. There is a clear difference between business exceptions, such as "the account does not have enough money in it" and technical exceptions, such as "the account database has only accepted one of the updates." System software, or middleware, should hide the messy realities of this machinery and present the user with interface services and protocols that don't require these issues be addressed in the business implementation.

Popular application servers, such as WebSphere or CICS, define groups of updates that must all be done together and enable the support of ACID services properties. As the transaction proceeds, the updates are completed and logged on a provisional basis. If they all work, the service can commit or synch-point the changes; that is, it can make them permanent. But if there are problems, the changes can be cancelled. If the system fails because of a power outage before the commit has been issued, it automatically backs out of the changes already made. The service's responsibility has ended, though the requester may need to resubmit the request once power is restored. The business service user is able to focus efforts on ensuring that business exceptions are handled. The technical exceptions can be safely left to the system.

ACID DESIGN CONSIDERATIONS

An ACID transaction should be "short."

In this context, "short" is a relative term. In a large system running hundreds of transactions per second, short would be less than a second. It's up to the designer to set a target for the duration of a transaction. In almost all cases, it's good to not allow characteristics, such as network latency or human think-time, to control the duration of an ACID transaction. This is important because it means that programs should not wait for remote input in the middle of a transaction, no matter how appealing it is to ask for user confirmation before committing. Applying resource-locking can provide a practical workaround. However, in distributed network architecture, such as SOA, that may likely exhibit asynchronous exchange characteristics, this also requires careful design consideration. A proven approach for minimizing the duration of locks on shared resources is to locally place the transactional services that update the shared resources on the same platform. This approach reduces latency between the services while simultaneously removing the risk of unreliability in the network infrastructure and creating the opportunity for local optimization.

ACID transactions should not be "big."

The term "big" is also relative. For example, a bad design practice would be to implement a transaction that corrects telephone numbers throughout an entire database due to changes in the national telephone

> **» SOA SECRET**
>
> In almost all cases, it's good to not allow characteristics, such as network latency or human think-time, to control the duration of an ACID transaction. This is important because it means that programs should not wait for remote input in the middle of a transaction, no matter how appealing it is to ask for user confirmation before committing.

> IN A SYSTEM WHERE THE TRANSACTION MANAGER, THE BUSINESS APPLICATIONS OR SERVICES IN SOA TERMS AND RESOURCE MANAGERS ALL ARE LOCAL, TRANSACTION MANAGEMENT CAN BE OPTIMIZED USING LOCAL PROTOCOLS THAT CAN HANDLE TRANSACTIONS MORE RELIABLY, EFFICIENTLY AND WITH GREATER PERFORMANCE THAN A DISTRIBUTED TRANSACTION MANAGER.

numbering plan. It should not be logically necessary to update the entire database atomically; that is, it would be better practice to update a subset of records, or rows, at a time and then commit the result before passing it on to the next subset. Otherwise, the transaction would effectively lock out all other users until the update was complete.

Transaction deadlock must be avoided.
In certain conditions, a state known as "deadlock" can occur. This is where two or more transactions are trying to access the same set of resources and each ends up waiting for the other to complete. For example, service A has updated a record with key *x* and then wishes to update a record with key *y*. Service B wishes to do the reverse. Neither can continue because invalid data would result. Ideally the system detects this and arbitrarily cancels one of the transactions. Since there is no actual error, this transaction should simply retry and start from the beginning. However, this is complex to implement when ownership of the resource is distributed between different application servers.

Complete isolation may have intolerable throughput implications.
There are cases with adding or deleting records where complete isolation may not be recommended. This is especially so in situations where all transactions are serialized. Therefore, systems typically provide the ability to relax the isolation property, allowing some concurrence while still preventing multiple concurrent updates to the same record.

THE ROLE OF MIDDLEWARE

The established practice is to delegate the provision of service characteristics to middleware, effectively absolving the business service implementer of responsibility for these characteristics and allowing one to focus on business requirements.

Middleware is a program or subsystem that manages or oversees the sequence of events that are part of a transaction and:
» enforces the ACID properties of a transaction
» abstracts transactional infrastructure services away from the application
» provides transactional coordination, such as logging and recovery, scheduling, threading, resource locking and concurrency, isolation and security

The middleware also provides value-added application functions such as:
» interfaced managed transactional resources, like databases and file systems
» systems management
» interfaced networks and other systems
» management of presentation interfaces
» an API for situations requiring fine control of transactions

Examples of middleware offerings that are helpful in delivering these characteristics are:

» application servers for J2EE-compliant business applications, such as the WebSphere Application Server
» transaction servers, such as CICS, for mixed language business applications
» database and data application management systems, such as IMS
» transactional relational database management systems, such as DB2 or Oracle
» reliable asynchronous messaging transports, such as WebSphere MQ and Citrix MetaFrame

TWO-PHASE COMMIT/ONE-PHASE COMMIT

Within a distributed transactional system, each system is either referred to as a resource manager or a transaction manager. The transaction manager controls the outcome of the transaction and is responsible for recovering resources. It also has to implement a recoverable logging mechanism to coordinate multiple resource managers, who apply the necessary network flows and logging procedure for transactional coordination.

A two-phase commit (2PC) is usually a prerequisite to supporting a distributed transaction. It may occur between an application server, a database or other transactional resource manager, like WebSphere MQ. A 2PC is an architected set of exchanges that transaction managers use to ensure that all resource managers in a transaction can be reliably coordinated, regardless of any failure. It's implemented by all transactional protocols.

A 2PC flow summary entails:

Phase one: The transaction manager asks all resource managers to prepare to commit recoverable resources. If a resource manager responds positively, it records the information it

needs and replies "prepared." It's then obligated to follow
through with the transaction.

Phase two: The transaction manger replies to each resource manager
with a commit flow. Upon receipt, the resource manager
finalizes updates to the recoverable resource and releases
any locks held on resources.

A single-phase commit (1PC) allows the decision to be delegated to the
1PC resource, allowing it to participate in a global transaction with any
number of 2PC-capable resources. In a 1PC, there is no recovery from a
communications failure. Applications using 1PC are subject to an
increased risk of a mixed outcome in a global transaction. Its transactional scope is often limited to a homogeneous environment. So, the
challenge comes when a 1PC occurs within a heterogeneous environment, as is typically represented by SOA composite applications. This is
one advantage of the centralized system with z/OS. It's uniquely optimized to implement a local protocol for handling transactions across
heterogeneous products like resource managers, databases, application
programs and transaction managers within a single platform.

In a system where the transaction manager, the business applications
or services in SOA terms and resource managers all are local, transaction management can be optimized using local protocols that can
handle transactions more reliably, efficiently and with greater performance than a distributed transaction manager. A centralized implementation for transaction management may use cross-memory protocols
for coordination. Further, these protocols may benefit from being
designed to accommodate fewer failure cases in the local platform
than in a distributed implementation. Several considerations apply
specifically to a homogeneous or a distributed environment, while
others are equally important for both. For example:

» A transaction's effectiveness is directly related to the number of
participants.

» Another general consideration is who coordinates the transaction. This may be a design issue or may happen by consequence.

» Effectively scoping the transaction during application assembly is a more difficult and error-prone task in a distributed environment since it may not be apparent which components have relationships with transactional managed resources.

» The requirement to avoid user interaction while locking is more significant in a distributed environment. The duration of a lock held while a commit is taking place impinges on the resources available to other applications. Fine-grained access of transactional services magnifies this disadvantage. Consolidating fine-grained distributed transactional applications into a more course-grained transactional business service, and placing it locally on the resource-owning platform, can return significant performance benefits and improved reliability.

XA AND RRS TRANSACTION PROTOCOLS

SOA applications often require concurrent access to distributed data that's shared among multiple components. Applications must maintain the integrity of data defined by business use under conditions of either distributed access to a single resource or access to distributed resources from a single application component.

In a distributed environment, the Distributed Transaction Processing (DTP) model is the most widely adopted for building transactional applications. Almost all vendors developing products related to transaction processing, relational database and message queuing support the interfaces defined in the DTP model. This model defines three components: 1) application programs; 2) transaction manager; and 3) resource manager. This model also specifies the functional interface between application programs and the transaction manager and between the transaction manager and the resource manager, which enables transactions with two-phase commit and recovery.

Another Distributed Transaction Processing Model

XA is an independently defined distributed transaction protocol adopted by J2EE standards. SOA applications that are deployed to distributed servers typically use the XA protocol for transaction coordination.

There are several performance implications in exploiting XA, including:

» XA requires a significant amount of network exchange between the transaction manager, the distributed participants and the resource managers. This is proportional to the number of participants in the transaction, increasing latency and introducing greater opportunity for uncertainty and unreliability, depending on the network transport characteristics.

» XA transactions require that the transaction context be propagated across systems with potentially disparate architectures.

» The XA API must be implemented requiring additional code and consequentially an additional application development burden for transactional management.

Additionally there are further considerations for transaction coordination in a distributed environment:

» A distributed environment may comprise a variety of platforms, transports and technologies with disparate reliability characteristics; there are likely to be a greater number of moving parts and interconnections, each of which introduces an opportunity for failure, delay or both.

» The potential for local optimization is much reduced.

» When system platforms or network infrastructure proves unreliable,

SOA applications that are consolidated onto a mainframe are able to use an » **SOA SECRET** **optimized local transaction protocol called Resource Recovery Services (RRS). RRS is a protocol used to manage transaction scope between different z/OS application environments and managed resources.**

A WELL-BALANCED SOA SOLUTION DESIGN WILL ADDRESS THE GOALS FOR CONSOLIDATING TRANSACTIONAL APPLICATION LOGIC AND DATA UPDATES TO OPTIMIZE FOR PERFORMANCE AND RELIABILITY WHILE MAINTAINING SIMPLICITY BY PROVISIONING FOR NECESSARY COMPENSATION TRANSACTION SERVICES.

transaction throughput can be compromised due to excessive roll-backs of failed transactions.

» It becomes difficult during solution design to completely capture the characteristics of each potential participant in the transaction with the consequence that the prediction of solution qualities of service may not be precise.

In a distributed transaction environment, using the XA protocol, there are many considerations for deriving quality of service for a particular application.

Resource Recovery Services

SOA applications that are consolidated onto a mainframe are able to use an optimized local transaction protocol called Resource Recovery Services (RRS). RRS is a protocol used to manage transaction scope between different z/OS application environments and managed resources. Within RRS, transaction protocol communications occur cross-memory instead of across the network resulting in greater certainty and reliability. Further, a single platform technology can be relied upon to manage the transaction leading to fewer moving parts and, perhaps, a more effective implementation.

The benefit of closely locating the transactional scope of the business application to the transaction co-coordinator on a single platform such as Z/OS is greater efficiency and simplicity in the implementation. This, in turn, leads to a greater throughput on highly concurrent resources and a guaranteed, predictable quality of service for the application.

The established design principle for transactional systems is to collapse as much transaction management as possible to a single transaction manager on a platform that is highly optimized for performance and reliability.

DESIGNING FOR TRANSACTIONAL SOA SOLUTIONS

SOA designers are faced with many technology trade offs. However, in order to improve the efficiency and throughput in processing transactional services, the following proven design practices should be adopted:

» consolidate physical tiers
» closely align applications and associated data onto the same physical tier where possible
» use distributed transactions only where necessary
» architect for clear and concise business service interfaces with granularity that matches the solution business requirements

In order to achieve the benefits of loose coupling and to achieve service **» SOA SECRET** separation appropriate for business design, the provision for business services must be partitioned so that the service interface boundaries are sufficient to meet the business requirements and optimize implementation efficiency. Best practices achieve this by maintaining transactional scope within one service implementation. In SOA, services are usually orchestrated to reflect an entire business process.

» implement business service interfaces by composing new and existing applications that reduce risk by maintaining proven qualities of service

In addition, an SOA design best practice is to:

» support reuse of existing trusted business applications in the construction of new services
» capture the purpose and value of defined services by applying good asset governance practices to reduce ambiguities

In order to achieve the benefits of loose coupling and to achieve service separation appropriate for business design, the provision for business services must be partitioned so that the service interface boundaries are sufficient to meet the business requirements and optimize implementation efficiency. Best practices achieve this by maintaining transactional scope within one service implementation. In SOA, services are usually orchestrated to reflect an entire business process. To achieve a balance between the needs for services with a well defined transactional scope and a reliable end-to-end business process, normally short-lived transactions may now be composed into sequences that implement a business service function which is an element of a long-lasting, enterprise-wide business process. To achieve this, design choices are needed that balance the requirements for performance and responsiveness with the need for reliability. Since reliability is a required characteristic, addressing this balance requires the design to implement what are commonly termed "business application compensating transactions."

Compensating transactions are a group of operations that reverse the effects of a previously committed transaction. They are used in several circumstances, such as:

» to restore consistency after an unrecoverable failure that prevented a distributed transaction from a normal completion
» when one of the global transaction participants in the enterprise

business process is a non-transactional resource manager

» when a long-lived business process transaction is composed of several atomic transactions

As an example, consider a line-of-business process created as a sequence of business service invocations, where each service invocation is a transaction that either completes successfully, or not at all. A travel application for instance may comprise business services for booking a flight, accommodation and a hire car. If the process is to be reliable, then, when an intermediate invocation of one business service cannot complete successfully, the business process is required to invoke the business service operations that will undo the results of any transactional service invocations completed in the sequence. So, if no hotel rooms were available at the destination then it would be necessary to cancel the flight reservation. This action is taken only when a series of retry attempts have been made and a business policy or user preference dictates its discontinuance. The scope of the process reversal, the flight cancellation operation in our example, is known as the compensating transaction and may extend either to all, or to a subset, of the prior service invocations; if it were not possible to reserve a hire car the user may choose to travel anyway and to select a different hotel within walking distance of the venue.

» **SOA SECRET**

The issue of security within SOA is more often viewed from a services perspective than as a data access issue. This creates significant problems with auditing regulations and requirements. In order to achieve required performance characteristics, distributed transaction managers often do not pass user information to the data access layer, but use generic user identifications to execute data access within a transaction.

In a long-running business process that is comprised of several atomic transactions, the boundaries handled by the transaction manager and those requiring compensation logic for failure cases must be determined carefully during solution design. The boundaries may be different depending on the transactional outcome. For example, the travel booking above comprises several separate stages; each stage may be an atomic business service transaction that has a well defined and reliable outcome. The process, however, may remain open for a significant time, days or perhaps weeks, while the user investigates options and makes choices. To satisfy the transaction design requirement for "short" transactions requires that the results of each transactional service are committed on successful completion. Determining the service transaction boundaries that address the requirements for atomic, reliable business services is an element of the business solution design. If the process is to perform, to have a reliable outcome and be viewed at the business level as a single transaction, compensation logic at the business service level will be required to undo committed actions in case of a failure at a particular stage in the process.

A well-balanced SOA solution design will address the goals for consolidating transactional application logic and data updates to optimize performance and reliability while maintaining simplicity by provisioning for necessary compensation transaction services.

ADDITIONAL DATABASE CONSIDERATIONS IN SOA

In distributed environments, where transaction managers and databases are located on different systems, it's common to use the database of stored procedures for common operations. This provides a consistent and secure environment in several perspectives.

First, procedures stored in the database are executed local to the data, ensuring transactional semantics while benefiting from all optimizations. The wide usage of stored procedures is an expression of the obvious benefit of co-locating business operations with the data accessed in that operation. Stored procedures can provide improved performance because of less network activity and related latency issues.

Another important consideration is security, since these applications and users have no access to the base data but can only execute specific stored procedures.

In addition, stored procedures enable the construction of highly optimized data access logic that resides in close proximity to the database. The advantage here is that the data access logic, implemented in the stored procedure, can be easily maintained in line with the organization of the database structure and provide for an abstraction layer that can be exploited by application business logic.

Furthermore, the performance of the stored-procedure layer can be highly optimized. Stored procedures, however, do not provide for a broad range of general purpose application services. Therefore, transactional application business logic should be implemented in a transaction manager or application server, such as CICS or WebSphere.

The issue of security within SOA is more often viewed from a services perspective than as a data access issue. This creates significant problems with auditing regulations and requirements. In order to achieve required performance characteristics, distributed transaction managers often do not pass user information to the data access layer, but use generic user identifications to execute data access within a transaction. Those generic user identifications accumulate the privileges that are needed to run any of the transactional services and become a

Another alternative is a shared-everything architecture, where all nodes have access to all data. This provides high availability and scalability by allowing access to the same data from multiple nodes.

» SOA SECRET

security risk. This is not what auditors require and companies complain that it doesn't meet their auditing and security requirements. If the transaction manager and the database are co-located, a single, optimized security mechanism can be used. Hence, security checks will not significantly impact required performance of the overall service execution. Penalizing security is the third highest reason why SOA projects fail.

The No. 1 challenge faced by SOA environments is to ensure performance and scalability. Performance characteristics of the database server very often determine the overall response time of the service as well as the system resources to serve the requests.

There are several architectural choices to enhance database scalability, high availability and workload balancing. One is a shared-nothing architecture, where several nodes are clustered together by a communication layer, with each node having its own portion of data. The application has a single-system view through the communication between the nodes. This architecture scales well with high parallelism but requires careful workload management planning and data placement. With data accessible to only one node, in a failover event, data is unavailable until the node is restarted. Those requirements are hard to fulfill in an SOA environment where data access demand can be very dynamic.

Another alternative is a shared-everything architecture, where all nodes have access to all data. This provides high availability and scalability by allowing access to the same data from multiple nodes. To gain those benefits while ensuring data consistency requires additional coordination between nodes. DB2 z/OS data sharing is one solution to this problem. It integrates hardware, operating systems and the database to communicate lock information between nodes.

SUMMARY

Using available tools, existing enterprise applications and data can be transformed directly into web services and reshaped into new business flows that exhibit the qualities of service required for reliable business processes with high performance. Web services are self-contained, modular, dynamic applications that can be described, published, located or invoked over a network to create products, processes and supply chains. They are built on open standards such as TCP/IP, HTTP, Java technology, HTML and XML. To put it simply, web services are building blocks that connect in almost any way to build needed processes and capabilities.

Transactional web services are the key to delivering reliable line-of-business processes. When incorporating application assets into new SOA solutions, reduced cost, risk and delivery time can be achieved whilst maintaining the performance, reliability and security that characterize the existing business systems.

Best practice in achieving these goals is to
» closely align applications and associated data onto the same physical tier
» reuse proven, reliable line of business applications as elements in the new solution so as to guarantee solution qualities of service
» architect for clear, concise business service interfaces that provide for well defined transactional scope with a service interface granularity that matches the business requirements

Maryela Weihrauch is a Senior Technical Staff Member with IBM USA. She has been working with IBM customers around the world to design their DB2 systems and applications for optimum performance and availability. Currently, she leads the DB2 Solution performance efforts in IBM's Silicon Valley Laboratory and drives DB2's enablement for service-oriented architecture. She consults in many customers projects with special focus on on-demand and SOA transformation. She frequently shares her experience and knowledge with customers as a regular presenter at technical conferences.

Steve Wood is product manager for CICS Transaction Server, IBM's industry leading transaction processing platform. He is currently responsible for definition, communication and execution of the strategy for CICS Transaction Server. He often acts as a product consultant to influential customers and key business partners and manages proposal, prioritization and commitment of product development plans. Wood is a chartered engineer with over 15 years experience as a software engineer specializing in communications protocols. He was instrumental in introducing TCP/IP implementation into CICS and co-invented CICS Web Support. Recently he has focused on improving the application development approach for CICS and drove the formulation and delivery of the new CICS Service Flow Feature in support of composed SOA application solutions.

Chapter

15

THE VALUE OF PROXIMITY

Deploying as many elements of SOA composite applications as possible in the same server operating image produces real advantages for the enterprise. This chapter describes these advantages and explores ways in which they can be realized.

BY MIKE COX & CARL PARRIS

A ll SOA services are, ultimately, composites of a variety of different elements. At a minimum there will be presentation logic, business logic and data logic. There will usually be interactions with elements behind the scenes that manage fundamental qualities such as the maintenance of a secure context and preservation of transactional integrity. If the service is a composite application that relies on the functionality of existing core business applications, there will be additional interactions with the transaction and data managers that own those resources.

SOA provides a great deal of flexibility in how all those elements are deployed in a physical configuration. At one extreme each element can reside on its own physical server. However, in our experience, the co-location of these elements in close proximity to each other, preferably in the same server operating image, facilitates several aspects of an SOA installation.

WHY PROXIMITY IS IMPORTANT

The primary reasons for placing the interacting application components of a service in close proximity are three-fold:

1. Reduce the latency for the interaction
2. Reduce the path length for the interaction
3. Reduce the management burden

Let's look at how proximity and optimizations can accomplish these
goals.

Latency

The primary reason for placing the interacting components of a service
in close proximity is to avoid the latency of interactions over a network
using TCP/IP. The application will suffer from increased latency any-
time a component's access to some other component for a needed
answer results in request and response flows across a network of
unknown quality. If the application is of low usage and well contained
so that poor throughput does not have adverse effects on other applications or shared system services, then an increase in server response
time of several tens to hundreds of milliseconds may never be noticed
by anyone.

However, latency is a major issue in high-volume environments. When
a unit of work is dispatched on a thread, normally the thread is
unavailable to perform another request until it finishes the original
request, even if the thread is suspended waiting for a remote service
to respond to a request. Network latency between components will
increase the amount of time that a thread takes to finish a piece of
work. This normally results in increased queue time for waiting
requests. It also normally increases the time that highly desired
resources are held, increasing contention for those resources, which
also results in additional delays to other threads attempting to access
these highly desired resources whatever they may be (e.g., database

rows, sockets, connections, etc.). Thus, modest latency growth for a single thread can be compounded to create negative systemic impacts affecting all threads. Simply increasing the level of thread concurrency often merely exacerbates the problem.

The network latency also can be aggravated by the need to establish the security context of the interaction between the two components. In order to protect the data as it traverses the network, additional flows are required, which increases the latency. In high-volume environments, where many things have to be accomplished within a short time frame, the number of interactions needs to be minimized and the elapsed times for the interactions must be tightened or latency can wreak havoc on performance and throughput.

When components are co-located, the code to access the adjacent component can be optimized to reduce the required number of information flows and to use a more efficient protocol or mechanism. Latency can be greatly reduced simply because there is no need for TCP/IP communications across a network or perhaps the TCP/IP flow can be eliminated entirely.

Often the underlying operating system environment can optimize flows to reduce latency. For example, a well-designed TCP/IP stack will detect that the two components currently communicating across sockets are actually in the same operating system. Therefore, it real-

> **When components are co-located, the code to access the adjacent** » **SOA SECRET**
> **component can be optimized to reduce the required number of information flows and to use a more efficient protocol or mechanism. Latency can be greatly reduced simply because there is no need for TCP/IP communications across a network or perhaps the TCP/IP flow can be eliminated entirely.**

THE PRIMARY REASON FOR PLACING THE INTERACTING COMPONENTS OF A SERVICE IN CLOSE PROXIMITY IS TO AVOID THE LATENCY OF INTERACTIONS OVER A NETWORK USING TCP/IP. ""

izes that it doesn't have to drive these requests out through an adapter loop, back in through that adapter and then back up the stack. The operating system can take advantage of that adjacency by reducing path lengths and eliminating part of the protocol, hence reducing latency.

In addition, the operating system and the runtime can take advantage of co-located components by optimizing communication flows. Application middleware, designed to recognize its operating system environment, can be tuned to that environment to take advantage of specific architectural and operating system implementations. In turn, this provides mechanisms allowing data flows between components without requiring TCP/IP and thus minimizing latency. In some cases, data movement itself can be avoided by simply passing pointers to the component of interest.

For instance, in communications from an application running on z/OS to DB2 on that same image, a local connector can be employed to move queries from one address space directly into a DB2 address space to initiate a database query. This eliminates the TCP/IP communication as well as the latency that would have occurred from the need to package a data transmittal on one end and then open it at its destination. Similarly, if WebSphere MQ is a participant in the application flow, messages can be placed on or retrieved from the queue directly without the need for a TCP/IP message flow. WebSphere for z/OS has an optimization which exploits z/OS cross memory services which allows IIOP flows between servers on the same operating system to avoid TCP/IP communication altogether.

Another advantage to this environment is improved security. Components can detect and acknowledge that they reside within the same operating environment and are using the same security mechanism; therefore, they use the same security context without re-authentication. In this way, security flows can be optimized by cutting out path length. User IDs and passwords do not need to flow across different environments that may, perhaps, create, modify or transform those identities as they move from one system to another. Using cross-memory communication techniques eliminates the need to establish an SSL connection, further reducing network flows and latency. Elimination of external TCP/IP flows also reduces the opportunity for security intrusion.

Elimination of a TCP/IP flow often results in a decrease in the instruction path length required to interact between two components. This is because the serialization and de-serialization of data to wire format can be avoided which increases the efficiency of the interaction which brings us to the next topic.

Path-length Reduction

High-volume systems are very sensitive to instruction path length. Well-written applications go to lengths to avoid doing expensive operations over and over. Many techniques are used to avoid expensive operations. For example, caching information that will remain constant for the life of the application instance, such as the host-

> Network latency between components will increase the amount of time that a thread takes to finish a piece of work. This normally results in increased queue time for waiting requests.
>
> » **SOA SECRET**

> **AN ADVANTAGE TO THIS ENVIRONMENT IS IMPROVED SECURITY. COMPONENTS ACKNOWLEDGE THAT THEY RESIDE WITHIN THE SAME OPERATING ENVIRONMENT SINCE THEY EXIST ON THE SAME SECURITY MECHANISM.**

name or pooling objects, which are expensive to create and destroy such as parsers, etc. In addition to application coding techniques to reduce the instruction path length, there are efficiencies to be had by placing components in close proximity. We will discuss two instances where proximity can lead to increased efficiencies due to path length reduction:

1. Proximity between application components
2. Proximity between the application and the data

Proximity of Application Components

The J2EE programming model facilitates the placement of the different application components of a service onto different tiers. Each of these tiers can be on different operating systems and on different hardware platforms. This provides the power to build composite applications accessing multiple backend data sources. Applications are sometimes deployed in a multi-tiered manner to avoid the impact of outages from middleware, OSes and hardware that do not have high availability characteristics. In other cases, components are distributed to avoid contention between high CPU-consuming transactions and high volume trivial transactions where the OS does not have the ability to manage the resource consumption according to a service level agreement's (SLA) determined priorities.

While the J2EE programming model and its connectors support the logical and physical separation of these components, there are significant performance gains to be made in keeping the logical separation while minimizing or eliminating the physical separation.

When the components are on separate tiers, several things can happen that impact the responsiveness and total cost of ownership of the application:

» increase in latency, or end-to-end response time, caused by the remote flow involving TCP/IP and a separate dispatch of this request onto a downstream tier

» increase in CPU cost associated with the serialization/de-serialization of objects into communication formats in order to pass the request to the next tier

» network bandwidth implications associated with the amount of data which must be passed from tier to tier

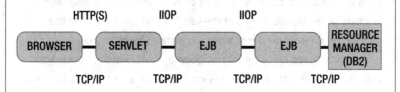

J2EE components largely interact through IIOP flows. A method call from a servlet/EJB to another EJB will likely involve the marshalling (or serialization) of the objects into a communications format, or a byte array, passing this array to the remote container, where the objects will be de-marshalled from the wire format (or de-serialized) and made available to the method call. The result set will then be marshalled back into a communications format and returned to the container of the caller, where de-marshalling will occur and the result set made available to the caller of the remote method. There are a number of data transformations and data moves in this process referred to as object serialization/de-serialization.

If the two J2EE components are in separate servers on different processors, this will require TCP/IP flows to pass the data in wire for-

mat between the two runtimes. This adds both CPU time and latency to the transaction. If the J2EE components are co-located in the different servers on the same processor, the inter-server communication can be optimized but the serialization and de-serialization costs are still incurred. If the components reside in the same server, the inter-server communication flow is eliminated. The runtime 'knows' how to invoke the downstream EJB without a TCP/IP flow and without a re-dispatch. This reduces CPU consumption and latency. However, the assembly and disassembly cost can remain. Some runtimes, such as WebSphere, support 'pass by reference' for objects residing in the same JVM when only remote interfaces are defined which eliminates the serialization and de-serialization costs.

The J2EE specification provides the capability of defining and using local interfaces for co-located components. Use of local interfaces eliminates the serialization and de-serialization operations as the method arguments, and result set are passed by reference, as opposed to 'pass by value.' It has been a "best practice" to design and use local interfaces when the components are known to be co-located. When this is not the case and that information is in two locations it is important to:

» Minimize the number of interactions between the web tier and the EJB tier, and
» Minimize the amount of data moved back and forth between these tiers.

In order to minimize CPU costs, latency and network load in this configuration, the application logic needs to be designed, or re-factored after the initial load tests, so that the answers to questions are passed between the physical tiers rather than just data that is then digested to form answers. Additionally, the size and number of the serialized objects, must be carefully examined. It may be necessary to provide the passed objects with a serialized and/or externalized interface implementation to reduce the amount of data passed across the wire and eliminate CPU costs associated with the default assembly and disassembly process in the runtime.

The potential performance benefits of re-factoring an application to avoid the costs of serialization/de-serialization can be illustrated by the experience the authors had working with an application for a large transportation company.

The following comparison was performed in the Washington Systems Center using a benchmark provided by a large transportation company for its customer information system. In Figure 1 the configuration shows the base case with the original configuration tested. The application flow consisted of a web container and an EJB container running in WebSphere on a pSeries box with AIX. The application servlet running in the web container made a local IIOP call to a session EJB which contains the business logic of the transaction. The session EJB then made several RMI/IIOP calls to data access EJBs running in WebSphere on z/OS which then accessed DB2 via Type 2 JDBC calls. In this case, DB2 is configured as a parallel sysplex for both scalability and availability.

The business logic session EJB was running remotely to the data access EJBs which executed the SQL calls to DB2. To make matters worse, for each transaction the business logic session EJB had to

In order to minimize CPU costs, latency and network load in this **» SOA SECRET** configuration, the application logic needs to be designed, or re-factored after the initial load tests, so that the answers to questions are passed between the physical tiers rather than just data that is then digested to form answers. Additionally, the size and number of the serialized objects, must be carefully examined.

make several calls to these remote EJBs. As a result, these RMI/IIOP calls added significant serialization/de-serialization overhead.

FIGURE 1 - REMOTE (DISTRIBUTED) BUSINESS PROCESSING LOGIC ENVIRONMENT

CLIENT WORKSTATION
WEB BROWSER
HTTP REQUEST

HTTP(S) DATA FLOW

pSERIES PROCESSOR
AIX OPERATING SYSTEM

WEBSPHERE WEB/EJB CONTAINER

« WEB REQUEST SERVICED HERE BUSINESS PROCESS EJB AND ALL BUSINESS LOGIC STEPS EXECUTED HERE

BUSINESS LOGIC INVOKES REMOTE EJB ON z/SERIES FOR SQL ACTIVITY

IIOP DATA FLOW   IIOP DATA FLOW

z990 PROCESSOR
z/OS OPERATING SYSTEM

z990 PROCESSOR
z/OS OPERATING SYSTEM

WEBSPHERE WEB/EJB CONTAINER

WEBSPHERE WEB/EJB CONTAINER

« EJBS FOR SQL CALLS EXECUTED HERE

DB2 SERVER

DB2 SERVER

DATABASE

Figure 2 shows the exact same physical configuration, but in this case, the application has been re-factored to place the business logic processing in the same EJB container with the data access EJBs in the WebSphere z/OS runtime. This significantly reduced the traffic from the pSeries machine to the zSeries machines. In addition, local interfaces were defined for the EJBs that shared the EJB container on z/OS. This reduced the number of remote EJB calls per transaction, significantly reducing the serialization/de-serialization cost.

FIGURE 2 - LOCAL Z/OS BUSINESS PROCESSING LOGIC ENVIRONMENT

CLIENT WORKSTATION
WEB BROWSER
HTTP REQUEST

HTTP(S) DATA FLOW

pSERIES PROCESSOR
AIX OPERATING SYSTEM

WEBSPHERE
WEB
CONTAINER

« WEB REQUEST SERVICED HERE
BUSINESS PROCESS EJB AND ALL
SERVLET INVOKES BUSINESS
PROCESS EJB ON z/OS PLATFORM

IIOP DATA FLOW   IIOP DATA FLOW

z990 PROCESSOR
z/OS OPERATING SYSTEM

z990 PROCESSOR
z/OS OPERATING SYSTEM

WEBSPHERE
EJB
CONTAINER

WEBSPHERE
EJB
CONTAINER

DB2 SERVER   DB2 SERVER

« BUSINESS LOGIC
EJBs RAN HERE IN
THE RE-FACTORED
CUSTOMER APP

EJB SQL CALLS MADE
HERE

DATABASE

High-volume systems are very
sensitive to instruction path length.   » **SOA SECRET**
Well-written applications go to lengths to avoid doing
expensive operations over and over. Many techniques
are used to avoid expensive operations.

Table 1 below shows that there was a very significant difference in the overall performance of these two application deployment approaches.

TABLE 1 - COMPARISON OF LOCAL VS REMOTE IIOP PERFORMANCE

BENCHMARK CONFIGURATION	AVERAGE CPU TIME PER EJB TRANSACTION (MS)	AMOUNT OF DATA TRANSFERRED PER EJB TRANSACTION (KB)
REMOTE (DISTRIBUTED) BUSINESS LOGIC ENVIRONMENT	11.73	54.4
LOCAL Z/OS BUSINESS LOGIC ENVIRONMENT	2.64	0.5

» AVERAGE CPU TIME PER EJB TRANSACTION WAS REDUCED BY OVER 77%
» NUMBER OF BYTES OF DATA TRANSFERRED PER EJB TRANSACTION WAS REDUCED BY 99%

By putting both the business and data access logic in the same WebSphere z/OS EJB container and minimizing the interactions between the web tier and the EJB tier, fewer cycles were spent in serialization/de-serialization and less data was transferred over TCP/IP resulting in reduced CPU consumption, bandwidth and latency.

Proximity to Data

While co-location of components has a positive performance impact in any Java runtime, the same is true for co-locating Java and non-Java components. In the case of DB2 for z/OS, in addition to the Type 4 JDBC driver, a Type 2 JDBC driver can be used when the J2EE components and DB2 subsystem reside on the same operating system image. When the Type 2 JDBC driver is used, the CPU cost of marshalling/de-marshalling data into a communication format and the necessary TCP/IP network flows are eliminated. With the Type 2 JDBC driver, the priority/importance of the current request being processed is maintained as there is no transfer of control to a different thread. In addition, the Type 2 (locally optimized) JDBC driver uses RRS for managing the transaction state, which has superior performance over the Type 4 (XA) JDBC provider.

This level of integration allows rapid and inexpensive communications inside the runtime and the operating system. On many distributed platforms two-phase commit is also handled in software somewhat external to the database commit process. With WebSphere on z/OS, two-phase commit is handled internally in the operating system using RRS. By integrating workload manager (WLM) for resource management and RRS for handling two-phase commit transactions directly into z/OS, rather than accessing it externally, an optimal proximity to data is maintained. On other platforms, resource management on WebSphere is done externally to the operating system.

The potential performance improvements associated with a change from Type 4 JDBC connectors to Type 2 JDBC connectors can be illustrated by a benchmark the authors were involved in for an application at a large financial institution.

The following benchmark comparison was done at the customer site using their configuration with the assistance of IBM. In this case, the

When interacting components are co-resident, management is **» SOA SECRET** simplified. Co-location of components means that these components are being managed by the same policies and in a similar way. When a company's servers are running the same operating system or are in the same operating system environment, they are all plugged into the same management infrastructure. This common infrastructure manages all the normal operations such as starting and stopping, component recovery and work rerouting when a component fails.

customer was running a multi-tiered configuration illustrated in
Figure 3:

**FIGURE 3 - FINANCIAL CUSTOMER WITH REMOTE (DISTRIBUTED)
ENTERPRISE DATABASE**

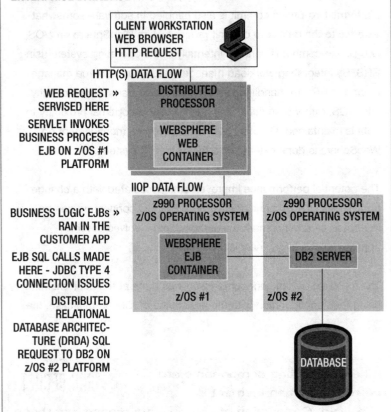

In this example, the WebSphere web container was running on a
distributed box executing a servlet that made a remote IIOP call to
WebSphere on z/OS. In turn, z/OS was running the session EJB business logic, making a local IIOP call to the data access CMP EJB
executing SQL calls to DB2 running on another zSeries box using a
remote Type 4 JDBC connection. This configuration was running

WebSphere on z/OS as a distributed tier, not taking advantage of the potential for closer proximity to the web container or closer proximity to the back-end data.

Figure 4 below shows the configuration when it has been changed to take advantage of local Type 2 JDBC access to DB2.

FIGURE 4 - FINANCIAL CUSTOMER WITH LOCAL ENTERPRISE DATABASE

CLIENT WORKSTATION
WEB BROWSER
HTTP REQUEST

HTTP(S) DATA FLOW

WEB REQUEST SERVISED HERE »
SERVLET INVOKES BUSINESS PROCESS EJB
ON z/OS #1 PLATFORM

DISTRIBUTED PROCESSOR

WEBSPHERE WEB CONTAINER

IIOP DATA FLOW

BUSINESS LOGIC EJBs RAN IN THE »
CUSTOMER APP

EJB SQL CALLS MADE HERE - JDBC
TYPE 2 (LOCAL) CONNECTION TO DB2
ON z/OS #1 PLATFORM

z990 PROCESSOR
zOS OPERATING SYSTEM
z/OS #1

WEBSPHERE EJB CONTAINER

DB2 SERVER

DATABASE

In this case the physical configuration has been modified to eliminate one of the tiers in the flow. The business logic session EJB still makes a local call to the CMP EJB, which executes SQL calls to a local instance of DB2 on z/OS using the local Type2 JDBC connection.

Changing from a JDBC Type 4 to Type 2 connector is a simple process of defining a new data source and configuring the application to use it. No change in the application itself was required.

Significant improvements in performance were observed as a result of this change. A 50% reduction in average end (web) user response times was reported by the test driver tools. In addition, the overall CPU required by the z/OS system environment was 50% less than the remote (two z/OS) system implementation.

When deployed locally with backend DB2 and transaction managers the WebSphere Application Server for z/OS offers opportunities for local optimization. The reduced processor consumption, improved response times and reduced bandwidth requirements combined with other quality of service advantages — such as resource management, transaction-commit scope management and security — make WebSphere Application Server for z/OS an attractive option for critical J2EE technology-enabled applications.

IMPROVED MANAGEMENT

The final value of proximity to be discussed is in improved management. When interacting components are co-resident, management is simplified. Co-location of components means that these components are being managed by the same policies and in a similar way. When a company's servers are running the same operating system or are in the same operating system environment, they are all plugged into the same management infrastructure. This common infrastructure manages all the normal operations such as starting and stopping, component recovery and work rerouting when a component fails. With a multi-tiered environment, if WebSphere on another platform accesses z/OS, a company would have two different tool sets and management environments that would have to be reconciled.

Moreover, the management component will be able to view all components at one time. It is not dependent upon agents to detect an anomaly and then pass it on to some other component (possibly on another box via TCP/IP) that can make a decision which would then be pushed down to other agents. All activity can be observed at once and corrective actions taken immediately.

Additionally, there is always the challenge of gathering and coordinating documentation needed for problem resolution, accounting, capacity planning, disaster recovery, etc. All of these activities require additional effort as the number of servers and platforms increase. There is a major management benefit of having many of the components of an SOA environment co-located. That is not to say that component co-location is a requirement for strong management. Companies can and do learn to manage any type of configuration. The question is how many moving parts can be optimally managed, how many management entities need to be knitted together to manage the total environment and how many skill groups need to participate.

SUMMARY

So there are at least two levels of proximity. One is when components just show up on the same operating system and/or processor but are not aware of anything else that may also be resident. In this case, while there is no real integration, there is the advantage of consistent management. If the underlying operating system is smart enough to identify co-residency, it takes advantage of that.

The other level is where the runtimes are not platform agnostic but are knowledgeable of the underlying operating system and its capabilities such as WebSphere for z/OS and other z/OS subsystems including WebSphere MQ, IMS, CICS and DB2. At this level, services are optimized to that operating environment for activities like two phase commit and logging.

The greatest advantages accrue if components are co-located, where the runtimes and infrastructure are cognizant of this co-location. If the runtime itself is cognizant of the operating system that it runs on, throughput efficiency will improve even more. More efficient protocols can be used without the application being aware of anything. All of this has to do with path lengths and the ability to drive a larger number of transactions with a given amount of computing resource to meet response time objectives.

The co-location of these components will address all of these concerns. Network latency will be eliminated, one management policy will control all components and everything will be under one highly secure umbrella. The value of proximity can be measured technically by latency and throughput metrics, financially by reduced operating costs, and in the peace of mind by having one security and one management policy.

Mike Cox is an IBM Distinguished Engineer working at the IBM Washington System Center in WebSphere for z/OS technical support. He has more thanr 25 years of experience in mainframe software systems. When not working with WebSphere customers, he can often be found on the open road riding his H-D Ultra Classic.

Carl Parris has worked in software performance on the IBM mainframe software stack for 20 years. His primary focus in the last 10 years has been on the performance of new application environments using Unix System Services, Linux, Java and WebSphere. When not working he can be found out on the water in any kind of boat that does not have motor on it.

AT A BOOKSTORE NEAR YOU

For more information contact:
Eric Green, Group Publisher
Phone: 914.244.0160
E-mail: eric.green@larstan.net
www.larstan.com

LARSTAN's THE BLACK BOOK ON

Not For Dummies

When You Need The Advanced Level Information